THE GREAT GRETZKY

THE GREAT GRETZKY

An abridged edition of
The Great Gretzky Yearbook

by

Terry Jones

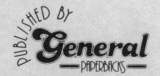

A Division of General Publishing Co. Ltd.
Toronto, Canada

The Great Gretzky paperback edition is an abridged edition of *The Great Gretzky Yearbook* published by General Paperbacks in November, 1981.

The Great Gretzky was published in January, 1982 by General Paperbacks
A Division of General Publishing Co. Limited,
30 Lesmill Road,
Toronto, Canada
M3B 2T6

Cover photograph by Brian Gavriloff, *Edmonton Journal*. Used by permission.

ISBN 0-7736-7025-4

Printed in Canada

ABOUT THE AUTHOR

Terry Jones, author of the original edition of *The Great Gretzky* in 1980, is the sports columnist of the *Edmonton Journal*.

Jones, who has also written the first annual edition of the book *Canadian Pro Football '81* and co-authored *Decade of Excellence*, the story of the Edmonton Eskimos of the '70s, joined the staff of the *Journal* in 1967. In 1972, he won a national award for sportswriting and became the *Journal*'s sports columnist in 1976.

A native of Lacombe, Alberta, Jones began his career in journalism with the weekly *Lacombe Globe* when he was in junior high school. He joined the staff of the *Red Deer Advocate* on a part-time/full-time basis while still in high school and became a member of the *Journal*'s sports staff on graduation.

Jones, who has won the Edmonton Press Club award for sportswriting each time it has been offered, covered the Edmonton Oilers in the World Hockey Association and the Edmonton Eskimos of the Canadian Football League as a beat reporter prior to becoming the *Journal*'s sports columnist.

A sportswriter who has covered such events as the Grey Cup, the Super Bowl, the Stanley Cup, Canada Cup, NHL Challenge Cup, World Series, Indianapolis 500, Olympic Games, Commonwealth Games, The World Figure Skating Championships, U.S. PGA and Bing Crosby golf tournaments, the Preakness, Boston Marathon and many others, also does twice-daily sports commentary shows on Edmonton radio station CHQT.

Terry and his wife, Linda, live with their son Shane and twin daughters Trina and Nicole in Sherwood Park, Alberta.

ACKNOWLEDGMENTS

Despite the gentle elbow in his direction in this book, I want to express my appreciation to Jim Proudfoot of the *Toronto Star,* for it was at his suggestion that I undertook this project.

A very special vote of thanks to Walter Gretzky for his kind cooperation.

My sincere gratitude, as well, to Cam Cole of the *Edmonton Journal* for his efforts beyond the call of duty in the editing of the copy. And to the many sportswriters — Jim Matheson, Jim Coleman, Ted Beare, Dick Denny, Tony Fitz-Gerald, Dick Chubey and Doug Milroy — my appreciation for their cooperation.

I'd also like to express appreciation to Ron Andrews of the National Hockey League and to amateur statistician Tom Barrett for their assistance in assembling the statistical section.

As well, thanks to Lynda Zerbe for typing the manuscript.

Special thanks to the *Edmonton Journal* and Colorfast, and photographers Brian Gavriloff and Bob Peterson who shot the majority of the pictures for the book.

But most of all, to my wife Linda and our three children many, many thanks for all the patience and all the understanding.

T.J.

THE GREAT GRETZKY

A young Wayne Gretzky, ten going on eleven, laces up his skates
(THE GLOBE AND MAIL)

CHAPTER 1

WHEN *THE KID* WAS REALLY A KID

The first goal Wayne Gretzky ever scored was during Hockey Night in Canning.

He beat his grandmother on the glove side.

His grandmother lived in Canning, Ont., and every Saturday night Walter and Phyllis Gretzky took their young son to visit her. While Walter watched Hockey Night in Canada on television, little Wayne Douglas Gretzky would take off his shoes and slide on stocking feet on the well-polished pine living-room floor.

"He'd stride and pretend he was skating like the players on television," remembers his dad. "His grandmother bought him one of those little hockey sticks that you find in souvenir stands. And he'd have that stick and a little ball. His grandmother would sit-in her big chair and she'd be his goaltender.

"By the end of the evening, she'd have bruised legs from getting hit with his little souvenir hockey stick."

Mrs. Mary Gretzky, his grandmother, was convinced that young Wayne would one day grow up to be another Frank Mahovlich, her favorite hockey player.

Sixteen years later, The Kid would bring her a picture of himself posing with his World Hockey Association All-Star team-mate, Gordie Howe. He autographed the picture with the message: "Sorry it's not Frank, grandma, but Gordie will have to do."

It was about 70 metres behind his grandmother's house, on the Nith River, that young Wayne, at age two, would take his first strides on skates. While he skated, his father, an amateur photographer, captured what someday should be a Hockey Hall of Fame movie of his son.

His grandmother was no longer playing goal, and, as time passed, she learned to remain at a safe distance.

"Wayne always had a hockey stick in his hands," recalls Walter. "I'll never forget the time Wayne's grandfather ad just replaced a window in his house that Wayne had broken with a shot. My dad had just completed the task of putting a new window in and he was standing back admiring his work when — smash! — Wayne took another shot at the side of his house and broke the window again. I can still see his grandfather chasing him with a hockey stick while his grandmother stood back and laughed her head off.

"His grandfather ended up putting a board in front of the window every time he figured we'd be coming over."

"Wayne kept us in the poorhouse repairing windows," remembers his mother, Phyllis.

The neighbor across the street from the modest house at 42 Varadi in Brantford, Ont., where Walter and Phyllis Gretzky live to this day, used to call the Ontario Provincial Police to report their son.

"Wayne always played ball hockey in front of the house and when the ball rolled across the road to her lawn, she'd call the police. The woman across the road was always scared to death that a car would hit him," Phyllis recalls.

No ordinary young man

Little Wayne Gretzky was never an ordinary lad.

Walter Gretzky describes his son, for all the years he lived at home, as being "quiet and backward." That isn't the Wayne of today. But he was bashful and so shy it was pathetic. He kept everything to himself. It wasn't until he had to move away from home and go to Toronto that he came out of his shell.

"One thing I noticed about Wayne when he was a young boy is that he never played with toys," remembers his dad. "He had all the toys any kid would want, but he'd never play with them. But give him a hockey stick or a lacrosse stick or a baseball bat, it didn't matter, and he'd be in his glory. He'd never get bored.

"I remember many times that other kids would come over in the afternoon and ask if Wayne wanted to go to a show with them. Wayne never cared about going. His friends would go to the show and he'd stay home, by himself, firing a ball at the wall until he'd knock the bricks out. Some days it would be 90 degrees out and he'd be out there firing the ball against the wall."

The place where Wayne Gretzky was happiest as a kid was the backyard at 42 Varadi in winter.

From the time Wayne was three, every year, Walter Gretzky would wait until the ground froze, cut the grass very short, and then get out the lawn sprinkler — which made for the most even flood — and turn the backyard, from fence to fence, into a 60′ x 40′ hockey rink.

January 1968 on the backyard rink, six going on seven *(WALTER GRETZKY)*.

His father had definite ideas

Walter Gretzky says he didn't push his kids into hockey, but he admits they were surrounded with the environment. And Wayne's father had some definite ideas about things.

"I believe in sport," said his dad, who for 25 years has worked for Bell Telephone in Brantford. "I believe that a kid who participates in sport ends up much more mature and much brighter than kids who don't. And they learn that if you want something, you have to work for it."

If there's one thing Walter Gretzky taught his son that he believes has shown up in his game, it's patience.

"Patience is one of his most underrated assets. He's like a vulture, the way he waits for somebody to make a mistake. When the other team doesn't make many mistakes, Wayne isn't that noticeable."

There were other things Walter believes contributed to the skills of his eldest son.

"I don't think I pushed any of the kids into sport. But I told them when they decided to go into a sport, I believed they shouldn't give it a half effort. Some people may say that's pushing. But I believe when you go into sport, you have to try to do the best you can all the time. I don't believe in the minor hockey philosophy that the kids should just be sent out to go have fun. To me, that's ridiculous. If the boy is sent out to do the best he can do, and he does it, he's going to be happy."

Track and field, Walter Gretzky believes, ought not to be overlooked in trying to determine just what it is that makes Wayne great.

"All my kids have participated in track and field and I think it provides something special for an athlete," said Walter, whose daughter Kim appeared to be on her way to national prominence in the sport when she slipped on a patch of ice and badly damaged her ankle.

"Track and field teaches you that you only get out what you put in. You learn how to excel within yourself. It builds self-discipline and it builds confidence. Nobody else is going to help you, only you."

Stereotype Canadian hockey dream?

It was the stereotype "Canadian dream." Backyard rink. Scrubs-on-skates to stardom. Except that most of the time there were pylons on the backyard rink — and that, some would say, is closer to the stereotype "Soviet dream."

Fifteen years ago, pylons were an unusual sight on a Canadian ice surface.

"I used to get a kick out of reading the stories about the European way of teaching hockey," Wayne remembered of the press surrounding the '72 Canada-Russia Summit Series. "My dad was teaching me that way when I was six."

Walter says he wasn't teaching anything in particular the Soviets did.

"But I guess we did a lot of things that weren't being done in Canadian minor hockey. You have to remember that in those times we didn't stress a lot of things we do now. All I was trying to do was stick to common sense."

The pylons?

"Possession is nine-tenths of the law," said Walter Gretzky. "The pylons work wonders for puck possession. Pylons and practice make perfect. The amazing thing, though, was that Wayne never got bored with skating around those pylons."

It wasn't always Wayne alone in the backyard, of course.

All the guys from the Nadrofsky Steelers used to come over. There were boys like Greg Stefan, Jimmy Burton and Lenny Hachborn. That was half a lifetime ago.

When Wayne Gretzky was en route to winning the scoring championship in the National Hockey League — breaking records many thought would never be broken — when Wayne, at age 20, was winning a second straight Hart Trophy as the Most Valuable Player in the NHL, the kids from half a lifetime ago were in junior hockey.

Greg Stefan was a goalie with the Oshawa Generals, Jimmy Burton a defenceman with the Windsor Spitfires, and Lenny Hachborn was with the Brantford Alexanders.

"We'd play in that backyard rink all day," said Stefan. "Eight hours at a time. There was a spotlight on it. We'd even play at night. There were hockey nets all around the yard, regardless of what time of the year it was. And all the guys on the team would go over there. We all hung around him when we were kids. He was a super guy. He didn't brag. And he's still that way.''

"At times it's hard for me to believe we were the same age and I used to play with him," says Jimmy Burton. "He's already done just about everything there is to do in the NHL.''

"I guess," said Stefan, "we've been friends and at the same time idolized him ever since we were kids."

They called him a 'hot dog'

While they'd certainly trade places with Wayne now, the kids who grew up with him, the kids who know how it was, wouldn't have wanted to, then.

''Half the time we felt sorry for him," said Lenny Hachborn, who scored between 150 and 160 goals playing with Gretzky on the Nadrofsky Steelers in 1971-72. "Back then, no, I wouldn't have traded places with him. He had all that pressure. Everybody was always out for him, slashing him. Even at that age. And there were all the problems with the parents who were jealous of how good he was. Most of the parents resented him. Now they're all bragging that their kids once played on the same team as Wayne Gretzky."

Jimmy Burton said it was never the kids.

"I felt sorry for him too. He was always picked on. And labelled a 'hot dog'. He was never a 'hot dog'. He was so modest, it was unbelievable. I know the three of us were never jealous of him. I don't think any of the other kids were either. I think we *depended* on him more than we were jealous of him."

"He wasn't a hog with the puck," says Stefan. "He set up plays like you wouldn't believe."

The three of them vividly remember watching Wayne, who scored an incredible 378 goals in 1971-72, cry after games.

"When we lost, he felt he was to blame," said Burton. "When he cried, nobody would say anything. Some of the other guys would cry too."

(WALTER GRETZKY)

Send, don't take, your boy to the rink

It wasn't easy, half a lifetime ago, for Wayne Gretzky.

"We, as parents, really get involved," said his father, Walter Gretzky, looking back on those days on the occasion of Wayne's eighteenth birthday, and trying to explain to Edmonton Oiler fans what it had been like for his son. "I do. I'm like everyone else. We lost sight of the fact it has to be fun for the kids."

Phyllis Gretzky still takes her kids to the rink. "But I learned a long time ago to sit by myself," she said.

Walter Gretzky doesn't talk about the harrassment his eldest son had to endure without first pointing out that "it was a small minority" and that "most of the people in Brantford were just super."

But that small minority...

"When I was coach, I could never take Wayne aside for even a minute without parents saying I was favoring him," says Walter Gretzky. "So I would spend the time with Wayne in the backyard."

After Wayne scored 378 goals when he was ten, going on eleven, his friends weren't the only ones feeling sorry for him.

"The fun left the game for him," said his dad.

"When I was twelve," Wayne admitted, "it ran through my mind. I thought of quitting."

At the age of fourteen, he left Brantford. Many of the reports, at the time, suggested it was because he wanted better competition so he could become a better hockey player.

"That was completely false," said Wayne. "The league I went to play in wasn't really any better than the league I could have played in at home. I just had to get away from the people. I didn't need it any more. It was really sickening. It really got to me."

"Many a time I saw him crying," remembers Walter Gretzky. "Some of the parents called him a 'puck hog' and a 'one-man team' when they won and blamed him when they lost."

"That's why I sit by myself now," says Phyllis Gretzky. "This way, I keep my friends."

There are dozens of examples of how it was.

Walter Gretzky remembers the day his team won the final game of a tournament 4-3.

"When Wayne came into the hallway outside of the dressing room, I asked him if he wanted a Coke. He said no. Kids always want a Coke. I asked him how come he didn't want one. He wouldn't answer. He just wanted to go. His eyes were red.

"You know what his coach told him after the game? His coach said to him, 'Do you have to be such a damn "hot dog" out there?' Wayne was never a 'hot dog'."

Wayne remembers a game he lost.

"It was the year I scored 378 goals. We lost a tournament final 3-2. I scored both of our goals. But we played our back-up netminder, who really wasn't very good. They had five shots on goal and scored on three."

It wasn't losing because of a kid who wasn't very good that hurt Wayne.

"The father of the back-up goaltender who played for us in that final game, came up to me after it was over and really lit into me. He blamed me for losing. I guess I should have laughed it off. But at that age, it really hurt."

Walter Gretzky, despite the fact Wayne's younger brothers have proven to have the same kind of magic touch, says the parents treat his other kids the way he wished they'd treated Wayne.

"I have to admit, I'm getting more enjoyment out of watching my other boys play hockey than I did with Wayne," he confessed.

The 'novice' who wasn't

Wayne scored his first goal — his only goal of the season — when he was five, going on six. At the time he was playing against players who were as old as nine and ten. Walter Gretzky, who fixes teletype machines for Bell Telephone, is an amateur photographer and he managed to snap a stop-action shot of Wayne's first goal. That was in 1967-68.

Wayne's dad kept the stats every season.

18

Wayne's second year of hockey, April 1969. He is second from the left in the first row. (*WALTER GRETZKY*)

When he was six, going on seven, Wayne scored twenty-seven goals.

The year after that, he scored 104.

In 1970-71, Wayne scored 196.

And then, the BIG year. Three hundred and seventy-eight goals.

"That was his last year in novice," said his coach, and uncle, Bob Hockin. "He should have been playing pee wee hockey then. It was just about the only year he played with boys his own age."

Hockin remembers it all like yesterday. The good and the bad.

"If we were losing, having a bad time of it, the parents were wondering why Wayne wasn't doing this and wasn't doing that. When we were up 8-1 or something, they figured he should be sitting on the bench most of the game so their kids could be on the ice more than he was. My feeling was that if he won games for us by himself one night, he should at least be able to play a regular shift the next night."

Not that there was anything "regular" about a Gretzky shift.

"He played defence most of the time that year," remembers Hockin. "Until, of course, the puck was dropped."

They loved to see him fail

"I remember one tournament we entered in Hespeler," tells Hockin. "Wayne scored fifty goals in six games. Almost every time he got the puck, he took it and went and scored with it. There really isn't any other way to describe the goals.

"But just as vividly, I remember the times when one of our kids hadn't scored a goal for a long time and Wayne would go through the whole team and then position himself by the side of the net. Instead of scoring himself, he'd position himself in such a way that he could feed the puck to the kid who hadn't scored a goal. He'd pass it to them all. The kids didn't have anything against him."

But the parents did.

"It was everybody," said Lenny Hachborn's mother, Lil.

"I felt sorry for him because of the way they'd boo him," she remembers. "They'd cheer if he was knocked down. You

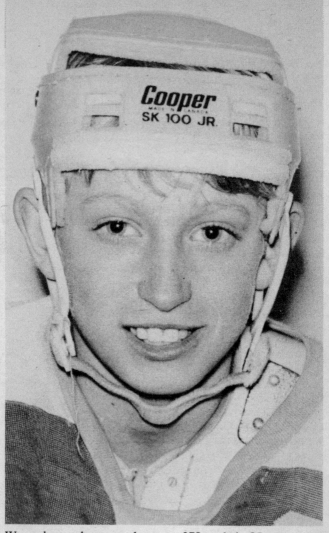

Wayne has a phenomenal year — 378 goals in 85 games *(THE GLOBE AND MAIL)*

could see it, every parent wanted to be Mr. Gretzky. A lot of people were always complaining that the team was only entering all the tournaments because of Wayne. They couldn't seem to see that their kids were on the ice too. And getting tremendous experiences out of it. It was really tough on the Gretzky family, especially Phyllis.''

Asked if she thinks Brantford deserves to have a black eye from it all, Mrs. Hachborn said, ''Yes, I feel that way. Brantford is certainly proud of him now but, in many ways, Brantford hasn't had all that much to do with where he is now.''

Most of that is water under the bridge to Wayne and his parents. The memories they, and everybody else, like to recall now are the good ones.

And it's difficult to bring up the name Wayne Gretzky anywhere in Southern Ontario without someone remembering a minor league hockey game they attended where he played.

Bob Wagner, who coached at that time in one of the largest minor hockey leagues in the Toronto area, remembers when the team his son played on had the experience of going up against Gretzky.

''My son played for the Cedar Hill Cougars in the Metro Toronto Hockey League,'' he said. ''And the team was considered a club of young superstars. They'd never been beaten. The club goes down to Brantford to play against Wayne Gretzky's team and loses 6-0. One boy stopped the whole team. He scored four of the goals and assisted on two others. The next time we played Brantford it was in our backyard and it was a different story. Our team led 8-0 in the third period and this kid Gretzky brings them back to win 11-10.''

The most dramatic memory Hockin has of Wayne involved his play in a tournament in Peterborough.

''We were playing Oshawa and we were down 5-0 in the third period and I was using Wayne all 60 minutes that game. Except in the third period, I pulled him off the ice for thirty seconds. It was the only time he was off the ice in the whole game. I told him, 'Wayne, you can score enough by yourself to win this game'. And he went out and scored six straight goals and we won the game 6-5.

"When Wayne was nine, he played for two teams: The major novice team for me and the minor novice team, mostly made up of nine-year-olds, his regular team from the other years, for his dad. We had him signed to two cards. After that year they changed the rules so a kid couldn't do that again. Wayne was playing for me in the Silver Stick tournament in Welland and in another tournament in Hespeler. But by the end of the weekend, his dad figured it was too tough on him. He decided Wayne better not come back to play with my team for our last game.

"But Wayne wanted to play. He finally talked his dad into letting him. He didn't want to let my team down. I'll never forget when we got the phone call. My team was down 2-0. The news just went through the rink like a prairie fire. Wayne is on his way! My players said, 'Come on, we can hold them down until Wayne gets here'. And they did. Walter carried young Wayne in from the car and dropped him over the boards. And we won both tournaments.

"It was a fantastic year, looking back on it, despite some of the things that happened.

"One night, I remember, we were playing a zone playoff game in Welland and a bunch of teenagers, some of them older brothers of players on the team we were playing against, decided that they were going to beat Wayne up. We had to get police protection at the rink and a police escort out of town."

The one game Lenny Hachborn loves to tell about was game in Grimsby.

"He scored nine goals and added nine assists," said Lenny, "Eighteen points!"

"I think the most goals I ever scored in one game was eleven," Gretzky admitted at one of his frequent interviews at the ripe old age of sixteen.

In 1972-73, in major pee wee, Wayne scored 104 goals. And the following year, also in major pee wee, he scored 191.

Signing autographs at age ten

On April 10th, 1974, Wayne Gretzky reached a minor hockey milestone.

As the *Brantford Examiner* reported the following day:

"Wayne Gretzky got the puck inside the Waterford blueline and let go with a slapshot. The Waterford goalie got a piece of the puck, but not enough to keep it from going into the net. Players rushed onto the ice and the game was held up for several minutes. Gretzky had scored his 1,000th career goal!"

"What would normally thrill a boy doesn't thrill Wayne anymore," Walter Gretzky was quoted as saying after that game. "But last night he was definitely thrilled."

The best memory the kids have from those days, is the year when they were pee wees and they got to go to the famed Quebec Winter Carnival in Quebec City.

"We only lost two or three games in the years we played with Wayne," remembers Greg Stefan, the goalie, who says he didn't get more than a dozen or so shots on goal per game.

"We had a lot of tournament wins. But there was nothing quite like the Winter Carnival trip. It was a wonderful experience for us. Wayne had received a lot of publicity. And we were used to having big crowds watch us play. But in Quebec City the papers were full of stuff about him before we even got there and there were photographers asking him to pose when we arrived. And the thing I'll never forget was that there were kids only a year or two younger than him, asking for his autograph.

"We played one game at 8:00 A.M. and the big coliseum there was packed. Everybody wanted to see him.

"He broke Guy Lafleur's record for the tournament."

Obviously, there were some comparisons made there with Lafleur. But mostly, people were calling him "The Next Bobby Orr." From the time he was six, he'd been called "The Next Bobby Orr."

But at the age of ten, when he was being followed around by a television network and major magazines such as *Sports Illustrated*, The Kid was making it perfectly clear that he had no desire to be the next Bobby Orr. He wanted to be the next Gordie Howe.

"Bobby Orr doesn't have any tricks," he was quoted as saying back then. "Not as many tricks as Gordie Howe. I like Gilbert Perreault better than I like Bobby Orr."

Gordie Howe was soon to begin to cross paths with Wayne Gretzky on a rather regular basis.

CHAPTER 2

"WHAT ARE YOU TRYING TO DO
TO MY SON?"

Gretzky had played his last game in Brantford and was about to head to the Young Nationals where he'd play on the same team as Howe's son Murray. How he became a Toronto Young National is something of an involved story.

Sam McMaster was the man in the middle.

McMaster, the general manager of the Nats isn't sure when he first saw Wayne Gretzky play. But, like Wayne's team-mates, he'll never forget the scene at the tournament in Quebec City.

"First thing in the morning and there were 13,000 people in a 10,000 seat stadium. The only place I could sit was in the aisle.

"I had gotten to know the Gretzky family over the years. I guess baseball had the most to do with it," he recalls of the sport which Wayne, to this day, maintains is his favorite.

"His dad, Walter, was helping schedule ball games and I phoned to schedule an exhibition game for my team. His dad wasn't home. And I started talking to Wayne.

"I asked him about his last year in bantam. He said it was lousy. He said the fans were all on his back. That his family was upset. And everybody was booing him. I told him if he wanted, he could come and stay with me and live in Toronto."

A few weeks later, McMaster received a call from Walter Gretzky.

"Walter was upset. He asked me what I was trying to do to his son," recalls McMaster.

"I said, 'What do you mean?'

"Walter said, 'He won't eat with us anymore!'"

Wayne had asked his dad if he could go live with McMaster in Toronto and his dad's first response was "No."

"I guess what finally convinced Walter that it was in the best interests of everybody was when Wayne asked him why he couldn't go live in Toronto and his dad told him that he was too young. Wayne asked how come he was too young, and his dad said he was worried that if he wasn't close to home, he might end up drinking or taking drugs.

"Apparently Wayne told his father, 'Dad, I can do that here. If you want I'll take you and show you where I can get booze and drugs'."

At that point, Walter Gretzky realized just how mature his young son had become.

"On August 1st," recalls McMaster, "I received a call from Wayne saying, 'I can come to Toronto'. I said, 'Good'. Then I had to find out if things were legal."

McMaster's first investigation left him convinced there would be no problem.

"I found no rule which prohibited it. And I went to the Brantford team and the president and secretary of the league gave me his release with no problem. They were 100 percent cooperative.

"He moved in with Bill Cornish on August 16th and he would live there and go to school and play hockey with our bantams. We put him under guardianship. But it wasn't because of anticipating any hockey problems. It was for the purposes of schooling and taxes.

"He played an exhibition game and there was no problem, but then I got a phone call from the president of the Metro Toronto Hockey League. He said, 'There's going to be trouble'."

The Ontario Minor Hockey Association said Gretzky could not play because he had not received an interbranch transfer.

"Bill Glover of the Metro Toronto Hockey Association said I needed a release from the jurisdiction called Ontario Minor. And they said they weren't releasing him.

"Everybody was telling me it wasn't worth my trouble.

Knowledgeable hockey men were telling me they'd watched Wayne in his final year in Brantford and they swore he was burned out, past his prime. They said he couldn't skate and that he'd never make it.''

McMaster explained the situation to Wayne.

''I told him we could try to appeal it. Or he could go back to Brantford. He said he wanted to appeal it.

''The first thing we did was go to court to try to get an injunction against everybody. But the court ruled, and rightfully so I guess, that we must try all avenues of appeal within the hockey structure before they'd hear it.

''We took the appeal to the Ontario Minor Hockey Association in October to their annual meeting. And they turned us down on the grounds that Wayne was moving strictly to improve his hockey. They said there was no exact rule, but their decision was made on 'the spirit of the rule'. There was a lot of press over this thing and almost all of the opinion and comment was in favor of Wayne playing in Toronto.''

But by this point Wayne had been out of hockey for five weeks. It was beginning to bug him.

''That's when I suggested Wayne go out and practice with the junior B team. Junior B came under different jurisdiction than bantam. It was legal for him to do that because now we were dealing with the Ontario Hockey Association. One day we were told, 'Yes, he could play.' The next day we were told, 'No he couldn't.' Then the day after that, 'Yes, he could' again.

''But everybody was laughing at us. Not only were there all those comments about Wayne being washed up at his age, but now they were saying we were going to hurt him. That we were doing the wrong thing for the boy.''

After one practice with the junior B team, Wayne decided that, yes, he could play at that level.

He scored two goals in his first game.

''Wayne was happy. His family had come up for the game and they were happy,'' recalls McMaster. ''And then at 2:00 A.M. I get a phone call from Walter. He told me 'They just suspended my boy'. The Ontario Minor Hockey Association had suspended Wayne for leaving without a release. He'd scored two goals and now everybody was mad. Walter

Wayne during his metro junior B season in Toronto *(THE GLOBE AND MAIL)*

worries a lot. But I told him: 'Walter, don't worry about it'.''

This time they won. And Wayne Gretzky began his junior B hockey career.

"He was the Metro Junior B 'Rookie of the Year',"
McMaster says matter-of-factly.

There was another boy involved in all the headlines with Gretzky that year. A kid by the name of Brian Rorabeck was in a similar situation. He continued the fight after Wayne jumped up to junior B. The appeal finally ended up at a tribunal, the highest hockey court in the region. It voted to allow him to play. Wayne, it turned out, could have played bantam hockey later that year. But by then he was doing so well in junior B, he wondered why he'd intended to play bantam in the first place.

The Wayne Gretzky Era begins

The second season with the Toronto Young Nationals was the only year of the five years he was away from home prior to his twentieth birthday that Wayne would not win a 'Rookie of the Year' award, much less whatever version of the Hart and Lady Byng awards the leagues had to offer.

"But that second year with us," remembers Sam McMaster, "was the start of the Wayne Gretzky Era."

It wasn't until the playoffs started that the Gretzky Era began. But he scored seventy-three points in twenty-three games in the playoffs.

"And it almost didn't happen. We were tied with Stratford at two games each and we were very close to losing out in the first round of the best-of-five playoff series. With ten minutes to play in the fifth game, we were losing 5-1. With four minutes left we were leading 6-5. Wayne scored four goals and added one assist in that span. We ended up winning 7-6 and Wayne had scored five goals.

"I really believe if we had not won that game, Wayne wouldn't have been rated in the top 100 players going into the draft. People didn't want to believe. If he'd been out of the playoffs early, he wouldn't have been drafted high. As it turned out he was the third pick of the first round by Sault Ste. Marie.''

McMaster has great memories of the Gretzky years in Toronto.

"I'll never forget his first goal in junior B. He went past the net. And all of a sudden the red light was on. I couldn't believe he scored from there. So I asked him, 'How did you score from there?' I'll never forget his answer as long as I live and I decided right then and there I'd never ask him about a goal again.

"He said, 'I shot it the only place it would go'.

"I mean it was a backhand over the goaltender's shoulder from the most incredible angle. And he viewed it as 'the only place it would go'."

Not only would Wayne get to meet Gordie Howe during these years, he'd meet a man by the name of Gus Badali.

"Murray Howe lived with Gus Badali," McMaster recalls. "Gus didn't know anything about Wayne. But he went to a few games when Murray was in the line-up and one day he asked me about talking to the Gretzkys about representing him."

Badali was then just getting into the business of representing hockey players. The Gretzky family liked his manner. And, when they got to know him, they were convinced he'd be the kind of agent who would be looking out for the best interests of their boy before looking out for himself.

Badali would almost become a member of the family as the relationship grew.

But it could have been Alan Eagleson!

"When we were having all the problems with Wayne's eligibility," remembers McMaster, "we approached Eagleson to be our lawyer. He told us he didn't have time to get involved with kids of that age.

"Wayne really looked up to Alan Eagleson. He liked to refer to him as 'The Eagle'. If he'd been our lawyer I think Wayne would have loved to have been involved with Alan Eagleson."

When Wayne played in the world junior tournament in Montreal against the Russians and kept winning the "Most Valuable Player" award, it was Eagleson who presented it to him.

"I think Eagleson asked him every time he made one of the

presentations if Wayne would be his client,'' McMaster laughed.

Gretzky had his agent by then, of course.

And he was playing for the Sault Ste. Marie Greyhounds, which by that time were being called ''Gretzky's Greyhounds.''

CHAPTER 3

THE SOO GIVES BIRTH TO NUMBER 99

He hadn't wanted to go to the Soo at first. "I hope it's Peterborough," Gretzky told Ted Beare, the *Brantford Expositor* sports editor, before the draft. "They're the best organization in junior A. I might not report if I'm drafted by a northern club like Sudbury or Sault Ste. Marie."

When the Soo drafted him, they were worried he might not report, as had happened to them previously when they drafted Pierre Larouche.

But Gretzky and lawyer Badali headed for Sault Ste. Marie to look the situation over and Gretzky decided to stay.

"It's friendly, more relaxed here," he observed at the time. "It reminds me more of Brantford where I grew up. I played junior B in Toronto for two years but I didn't see much of my team-mates between games."

Gretzky didn't waste any time convincing the doubters as he stepped into junior A hockey at sixteen. In his first exhibition game against Sudbury, Gretzky stole the show. He had a goal and five assists.

Sault Ste. Marie sportswriter, Alex Mitcheli, captured a dressing-room scene after Gretzky scored three goals and three assists to lead the Greyhounds to a 6-1 win over Oshawa Generals in their league opener. Gretzky had received a bottle of Brut as his reward for being named player of the game.

"What's this Brut stuff?" Gretzky asked his team-mates.

"It's after shave lotion," said Greyhound Doug Kimbell.

"After shave lotion," said Wayne. "What am I supposed to do with after shave lotion?"

Two years later, with Gretzky in the National Hockey League, agent Badali would say, "I kid him every day that I wish he'd start shaving so we could get an after shave commercial for him."

Gretzky's coach for the first half of the season in Sault Ste. Marie, until he was replaced by Paul Theriault, was gregarious Muzz MacPherson.

And, oh, the memories he has.

Wayne poses with Greyhounds' coach Muzz MacPherson *(BOB FROST, SAULT STE. MARIE STAR)*

Number 9 was taken

"I'd never seen him play," said MacPherson. "And we picked him third. All I'd heard about him was that he wasn't very big and that there was some question about his skating. A couple of scouts, Fred Litzen and Fred Smith, sat with me one night at the Royal York Hotel in Toronto and said 'relax'.

"It didn't take long for me to be impressed with Wayne. The first time I met him was in a hotel room at the Royal York and he was a kid who knew where he was going. Exactly.

"He and his agent, Gus Badali, were hesitant to come to The Soo. They were concerned about ice time. I couldn't guarantee ice time. But I told him we had Craig Hartsburg on the team and the year before was his rookie year with us and he received more than his share of ice time.

"And Wayne had ice time when I was the coach at Sault Ste. Marie. I used him everywhere. I used him on the power play, when we were short-handed, when we were two men short, and the *Sault Ste. Marie Star* was constantly criticizing me for the ice time I gave him. They criticized me because they figured I was burning him out.

"All I know is that when you've got a good hockey player, you use him. I was criticized to death for burning him out. Let me tell you, the guy who is getting the last laugh out of Wayne's career, is me!"

Muzz MacPherson is the man who gave the Great Gretzky the now famous Number 99.

"Brian Gualazzi was on our team the year before and he'd worn number nine," MacPherson remembers. "Wayne wanted number nine. I told Wayne that Brian had the number. If he wanted to give it up, fine, Wayne could have it. But I wasn't going to take it away from him.

"I asked Brian about it, and he said he didn't want to give it up. Not unless he had to.

"So Wayne decided he'd wear number 19.

"I told him that with Phil Esposito and Ken Hodge joining the New York Rangers and deciding to take numbers 77 and 88 respectively, maybe he ought to consider going up by 11 more and taking 99.

"Wayne was really worried that people would laugh at him if he wore number 99. But I convinced him to try it. They didn't laugh at him."

"I know they expect another guy like Bobby Orr," Gretzky said, at the time, explaining what fans expected of him. "But this is just my first year of junior A hockey. I'm still young. I don't control a game like Craig Hartsburg, but when I get to his age, when I'm eighteen, maybe I'll be good enough to control it."

Number 99 poses for this shot during his year with Sault Ste. Marie Greyhounds *(MARGARET CAMERON, SAULT STE. MARIE STAR)*

'It was more hectic when I was ten''

The press attention, in Wayne's year at The Soo, was even greater than it was the year he scored 378 goals in the season he started as a ten-year-old and ended as an eleven-year-old.

Sports Illustrated was following him, the *New York Times* was following him, and he'd spend as long as an hour and a half in the dressing room talking to reporters after games and had to take cabs to get back to the hotel.

But by this time Wayne was an old pro with the media.

One day, he even started to fight back. When *The Weekend Magazine* put in a request to interview the sixteen-year-old, Gretzky agreed but only if it was at 9:30 A.M. and the writer would buy him breakfast. It was the only way he figured he'd get a meal that day. Following the interview he had to meet with a reporter from the *Toronto Sun* and then a reporter from the *Toronto Star* and then he had to show up for film features for television station CBLT and Hockey Night in Canada.

"Really it's not all that bad," Gretzky said that day. "It was more hectic when I was ten."

"At first," recalls MacPherson, "the other players' noses were out of joint. I'd be lying if I said they weren't. But they got used to it. And after a while, watching him be interviewed endlessly, I think there were times they were glad they weren't in his shoes.

"The thing that stopped them from resenting Wayne, though, was that they saw that none of it went to his head.

"The only time he did the 'I'm Wayne Gretzky' routine was funny as hell.

"It was our rookie initiation.

"The year before, in Hartsburg's rookie year, the players made the rookies streak down Queen Street with absolutely nothing on, except for a hockey sock over their heads so nobody would recognize them. I got to meet the mayor of Sault Ste. Marie over that one.

"The next year I decided I'd better get involved in the rookie initiation. Without the rookies' knowledge, of course.

"We set up the same thing. Except that we involved the police in this one.

"All the rookies were in one car, eight of them, and they

were all in jockey shorts and nothing else. Wayne was one of the rookies. And just as they were to go streaking, the police car pulled up.

"Wayne thought he could get all of them out of a jam so he jumped out of the car. And he said, 'I'm Wayne Gretzky'.

"The policeman looked at him and said, 'No, you're not. You can't be Wayne Gretzky. I know Muzz MacPherson and I know that he doesn't associate with fags. So you can't be Wayne Gretzky'.

"Wayne didn't know what to say. But I think that made him think about saying 'I'm Wayne Gretzky' after that.

"But he was unbelievably modest. And by Christmas all the resentment had disappeared.

"There's a difference between modesty and dedication to the game, though. I remember once we were on the road and Mike Boyd was giving him a rough time about being glued to a Hockey Night in Canada game on television.

"Boyd told him he didn't have to study the game so hard because it would be four years before he'd be in the NHL.

"Wayne gave him a pretty good shot. He said Boyd didn't have to watch the game because they don't televise games in the 'I'. The 'I' stands for the International League.

"I knew Wayne wouldn't be in The Soo for four years. No way."

MacPherson said the other thing that helped Wayne fit in was his sense of humor.

"One night we got beat. Really got beat. I was fuming. When we got home at 3:00 A.M. I made the team go out and skate in the arena with their suits and ties on. All I let them change was their shoes for skates. I made them skate in their suits and ties for forty-five minutes. In the dark.

"The next night we won 8-2. And Wayne, noting that coaches tend to follow the same routine during winning streaks, came up to me after the game and said, 'Gee, coach, I hope you're not superstitious!' "

And, of course, you had to have a sense of humor some nights after playing against Gretzky.

Gary Green, who would later become the coach of the

Washington Capitals, came up with an ingenious plan one night to slow Gretzky down.

He informed his players that he would reward them with $2.00 for each hit on Gretzky.

"Some guys had visions of making $50.00," said Green, "but little did they know Wayne Gretzky. All I paid out that night was a buck. Paul MacKinnon had half a hit."

Gretzky sets to rifle a shot at the net after pulling the netminder out of position *(KEITH STEPHEN, SAULT STE. MARIE STAR)*

The top rookie

Wayne was hot in his rookie year with the Greyhounds. In September, Gretzky scored seven goals and added eight assists — in only four games — for fifteen points. In October, in eleven games, he scored eleven goals and twenty-one assists for thirty-three more points. In twelve games in November, he scored fourteen goals and added twenty-one assists for a thirty-five point month. In the five games during December, he added four more goals, nine more assists and thirteen more points. With sixteen goals and twenty-two assists for thirty-eight points, he had his best month in the thirteen games of January.

He came up with his 100th point on January 3rd. His 50th goal on January 28th in Kitchener. His 100th assist on March 10th. In one game, against Windsor, he'd put together seven assists.

And, with a little fatherly advice, he broke the goal scoring record by a rookie.

"My dad told me not to worry about it. He told me the element of surprise could now work for me," Wayne laughed in the post-game dressing room.

Gretzky's parents were among the 4,017 spectators at the Memorial Gardens to watch their son score twice and add two assists in an 11-1 trouncing of Kingston which snapped a four-game goal scoring drought and enabled Wayne to tie the record for goals by a rookie at sixty-seven. He would end up with seventy goals, 112 assists and 182 points to finish second to Ottawa's Bobby Smith.

Gretzky won the Emms Family Trophy for being the league's top rookie and the Bill Hanley Trophy for being the league's most gentlemanly player.

At the end of the season the question was being raised: Had Sault Ste. Marie seen the last of Wayne Gretzky in a Greyhounds' uniform?

Wayne had discussed the possibility of going elsewhere in January at the World Junior Tournament in Montreal.

"At the moment," he was widely quoted as saying, "I would consider it very unlikely that I will play four more years of junior hockey before turning pro. I think I need one more

Wayne ties the goal scoring record for a rookie in OHA Junior A play with goal number 67 *(KEITH STEPHEN, SAULT STE. MARIE STAR)*

year of junior hockey, a year to grow physically and learn a little more hockey. But by then, I would have a reputation and I think I would be a sitting duck for other players to make a reputation at my expense. I don't want that to happen. There's just too much chance an injury could finish me off before I ever get a chance at the pros. I could go over to Sweden for a couple of years. The risk of injury wouldn't be so great and it would be a good learning experience for my hockey skills. I could play over there for two years and then come back to the NHL when I was eligible.''

There were reports that Wayne was unhappy about the amount of school he'd missed.

But it was more than that.

"Wayne is upset with his ice time," said general manager Angelo Bumbacco making reference to the fact that when Theriault took over as coach on February 21st when Mac-Pherson was fired, one of his first priorities was to reduce Gretzky's ice time by as much as ten minutes per game.

MacPherson contends that "Wayne almost went home when they let me go as coach" and he says Wayne Gretzky was the guy who got him the new job as coach of the New Westminster Bruins, owned by Nelson Skalbania, the man who was soon to sign Gretzky to a pro contract.

"I'm convinced I'm in New Westminster because of Wayne Gretzky."

He also figures Wayne would have stayed in The Soo one more year if he were still the coach.

"There's no question about that," MacPherson says. "His dad once told me if I'd stayed, Wayne would have stayed there for another season."

MacPherson's favorite on-ice memory of Gretzky was on Team Canada in the World Junior Tournament in Montreal that year.

"I've seen him score a lot of beautiful goals but he scored one, making a move on a Soviet defenceman, that I can't even describe," he said.

Gretzky impressed more than a few people in that tournament.

He made a believer out of Team Canada co-coach Orval Tessier for one.

"I was skeptical about Gretzky, not having seen him play except once in his own league," said Tessier at the time. "But he's certainly convinced me and everyone else now. He's very intelligent. He has a tremendous amount of puck sense. He's a pleasant surprise."

Gus Bodnar, a former Oshawa Generals coach, took his turn behind the bench and needed no convincing.

"Gretzky's always played two years above his class," said Bodnar at the tournament. "He's just amazing."

CHAPTER 4

THE KID WHO ENTERED THE WORLD HOME FOR THE AGED

When it happened, when Wayne Gretzky signed with the World Hockey Association, it was swift and sudden. It certainly didn't come with the sort of publicity buildup there was over Bobby Hull jumping from the NHL to the WHA. It came with almost no press speculation. The timing of Gretzky's signing was impeccable.

When Nelson Skalbania parked his private jet at Edmonton Industrial Airport at 4:00 P.M. on Sunday, July 11, 1978, and introduced Wayne Gretzky, signed, sealed and delivered for his Indianapolis Racers World Hockey Association franchise, it was perfect.

Twenty-four hours earlier an eighteen-year-old jockey by the name of Steve Cauthen had won his first triple-crown. And twenty-four hours later the NHL annual meetings would begin in Montreal. Skalbania wasn't at all subtle about it. He stopped the plane in Edmonton to announce the story because he wanted the news to get out right then and there. He wanted the NHL owners to swallow their cigars at the meetings.

If there was any inclination to start screaming about the age of the kid Skalbania had just signed up, one had only to think of Cauthen. If there was a Major Junior Jockey League, where would Steve Cauthen be? Riding for $75 a week in Sault Ste. Marie, Kentucky? Besides, Bobby Orr had been an underaged junior. Gordie Howe had been an underaged junior. Why not Wayne Gretzky?

At the time, WHA merger hopes had just been scuttled

again. And the signing of Gretzky... Well, all's fair in love and war — and the war had just been declared again. Even on day one of Gretzky's pro career, the smart money was saying he was going to be the WHA's hole card for merger.

The teenager from Brantford, the most touted young hockey player and the most eagerly anticipated genius of the national game since Orr, was suddenly a millionaire at seventeen.

A seven-year contract and a dream come true

And there he sat, in the crowded private jet of Vancouver-based entrepreneur Skalbania, fingering a cheque for $50,000 — a mere down payment on a seven-year personal services contract estimated to be worth $1.75 million.

"I guess the master plan worked," said Gretzky on the plane as he talked to the *Edmonton Journal*'s Jim Matheson in an exclusive interview. "The dream's come true."

Gretzky had contracted to work for Skalbania wherever the owner might go. "Who knows," laughed Skalbania, "he might end up as a deckhand on my boat in the Mediterranean."

The signing, which was completed on a flight from Vancouver to Edmonton with Gretzky's agent, Gus Badali, and Walter and Phyllis Gretzky, was precipitated by Skalbania's dislike for the owners in the National Hockey League. There was no doubt about that. It was rather ironic that two years later, Skalbania, who once owned the WHA Oilers before selling half the team (and finally all the team) to Peter Pocklington, would be one of them as a result of his purchase of the Atlanta Flames and the relocation of the franchise to Calgary. But that was to be another movie.

"I don't really know if this will kill any talk of merger between the two leagues or not," said Skalbania. "But I do know that I didn't like going on my hands and knees begging to get into the NHL last year. Who knows, maybe they'll call a truce now and say enough is enough. The situation, now, is just ridiculous."

Gretzky, six months later, was still marvelling at how he got that first contract from Skalbania, and how crazy it was in the plane, as the deal was struck on that flight from Vancouver to Edmonton in the summer of 1978.

"I had to write it," said The Kid. "I was handed a crumpled sheet of paper. Gus was talking, my dad was too nervous and Skalbania said he couldn't write it because he said the figure made him dizzy."

But the whole thing wasn't a spur of the moment affair on Skalbania's part. Not a bit. Didn't he call a couple of Edmonton media men the night before to ask them if they thought it was a good idea? And he certainly didn't sign the youngster without having watched him perspire.

Skalbania is a noted jogger. He decided he wasn't going to sign an athlete for $1.75 million without at least checking him out to see if he was sound. Skalbania asked Gretzky if he'd like to go for a run. It turned out to be a six-and-a-half-mile marathon.

"It wouldn't have been too bad," said Gretzky. "But it was uphill most of the way."

Gretzky, once a notable Ontario high school runner in the 800 and 1,500 metres, as well as a cross-country competitor, passed with flying colors. Even at this stage of his career, it couldn't be said that he took the money and ran. Skalbania saw to it that he ran before he took the money.

And the money wasn't easy to get used to.

"I still find it hard to believe," Walter Gretzky was saying six months later. "I've worked twenty-two years for Bell Canada and I've never been able to save much money. Now, at seventeen, look how much Wayne has."

But now it was Indianapolis's turn to get to know Gretzky. After the brief stop in Edmonton, the plane continued to Indianapolis where a press conference was to be held the next day.

The signing shook all of hockey

Wayne Fuson, sports editor of the *Indianapolis News* wrote, "The impact of the signing will be to Canadian hockey what Charlie O. Finley's attempted sale of Vida Blue to the Cincinnati Reds was to American League baseball."

A few weeks later, in an interview with *Indianapolis News* hockey writer Dick Denny, Gretzky admitted he felt that impact.

Wayne during a light skate with the Indianapolis Racers (*BOB DOEPPERS, THE INDIANAPOLIS NEWS*)

"I knew I would get criticized when I signed with the Racers. When I made my decision to leave junior hockey, I knew I had to stick with it. I don't have any regrets," he told Denny. "All in all, though, I guess my decision really shook Canada. I guess you'd say I'm pretty well known but not as much down here. I was ready for the criticism. I knew it would hit hard. But not that hard. They said I should have waited until I turned twenty."

Gretzky, who took the Indianapolis media men by surprise with the way he handled questions ("I've been interviewed all the time ever since I was six," he had to explain), was introspective enough.

"There will be quite a difference when I start the season, won't there?" said Wayne. "Men! I'll be playing against men. But I don't feel any different when I go onto the ice. Away from the rink I'm not any different than any other teenager."

Back in Canada the media wasn't so concerned with a minor thing like that. There was outrage from the media men who had the NHL logo tattooed on their behinds.

"A lot of people have said I was foolish not to be thinking of playing sometime in the Stanley Cup playoffs," Gretzky would answer. "But right now the NHL is just going on prestige. It's good. But who is to say it's better than the WHA? I think the WHA has proved to be of equal calibre to the NHL."

Gretzky, after the Indianapolis press conference, would return home to take power-skating lessons. People were still saying he couldn't skate.

"Everything taught in power-skating lessons is designed to help you at some time or another," Gretzky would later explain. "All the Europeans are taught to skate the same way. In Canada everybody learns differently. Power skating helps your strength, balance, and agility and I figured it would improve my acceleration — or starting from a standing position — which was the weakest point of my skating."

When the season started all eyes, as always, would be on Gretzky. Except, of course, Gretzky's. He remembers noticing Robbie Ftorek, the 5'8", 155-pound star of the Cincinnati Stingers.

"After seeing Ftorek, I couldn't help but wonder why

everybody was cutting me up about my size,'' said The Kid, who was then 5'11" and 164 pounds.

Gretzky "only" managed three goals and three assists in his eight games in Indianapolis.

He had two big nights, though.

In one game he scored a goal and added two assists against the Birmingham Bulls. But those statistics were secondary to the bottom-line statistic. The million-dollar baby played that night before a crowd of 1,919 fans in Indianapolis.

Dave Overpeck of the *Indianapolis Star* lectured the fans after that one: "If you are a sports fan at all," he wrote, "you owe it to yourself to come out and watch Wayne Gretzky play hockey. A generation or so from now, you'll be able to tell your grandkids, 'I saw him when he broke into the majors as a seventeen-year-old kid'."

When the Edmonton Oilers came to town, Gretzky scored two goals.

It was interesting, at that moment, to view Gretzky. The first look, of course, was to see if there were any signs of money spoiling the kid. But no matter how hard you looked, it just wasn't there. He may have been worth almost $2 million, but he was still wearing faded blue jeans and sneakers. He was still going to night school twice a week. Still in a room-and-board situation and still living on an allowance of $100 a week. If his Racer team-mates didn't jokingly call him "Brinks," you'd never know he was a millionaire.

"I'm trying to live like any normal seventeen-year-old kid," he said. "I'm living with a family just like I did in junior for two years. I'm enjoying where I'm living. Next year, maybe, I'll live on my own, but now..."

Gretzky was living with Dr. Terry Fredericks and his family. And he was still going to grade twelve, attending classes at Broad Ripple High School where he was taking economics and American history.

"The students don't know that much about who I am right now and I'm trying to keep it down as much as possible," he said. "I want to be treated just like anybody else."

That wasn't much of a problem at the Frederick's residence on Windsor Drive in Carmel, Indiana. "I don't think anybody on the block really knew who he was," said Dr. Terry Fredericks. "It was kind of like he was an exchange student. In our area, people didn't follow hockey that much."

One neighbor knew who he was — Don LeRose, the general manager of the Racers. Fredericks happened to be at his house when LeRose had to find a place for Wayne to board.

"We didn't have a teenager in the family," said Sherry Fredericks. "He was just super with our youngsters, Jeff, Brett and Amy. He just fit right in with the family. It was a joy. And not because he was a young superstar. Because he was such a nice young person."

"But the grocery bill was considerably higher than we expected," said Dr. Fredericks. "We couldn't keep him filled up."

Mature beyond his years

The only luxury Gretzky had permitted himself was a Trans-Am car. And even that surprised people. Why not, for example, a Corvette?

"Gus has me on a weekly allowance," said Wayne at the time. "It's not more than any seventeen-year-old would get." Well, maybe a little more?

And, oh yes, there was no girlfriend.

"I'm only seventeen," said Wayne. "And because I've been in four different cities in the last four years I don't have time for a special girl. I have always been taught by my parents to determine my priorities and make sure that they are set. Then you can always have the social life on the side. The girls will always be there."

Now that was maturity!

"The sudden wealth hasn't gone to Wayne's head," said coach Pat Stapleton. "He's had the notoriety for a longer period of time than most kids because of his exploits as a youngster. Wayne came from a humble background. His parents did a good job bringing him up."

"He's mature beyond his years," said Racer team-mate Dave Inkpen.

And on the ice...

"Big league hockey is a lot like I expected," Gretzky

(BOB DOEPPERS, THE INDIANAPOLIS NEWS)

reported. "Of course, the players are a lot older than in the junior league and a lot more mature. They think a lot faster. They skate a lot faster. And they are a lot stronger. A guy my size and my age has to go out there and outthink them and outsmart them. I've got to use brains instead of brawn."

"He's not going to be a star overnight."

Despite the fact Indianapolis wasn't exactly filling the rink to watch him play — something of a first in Gretzky's career — and that he wasn't exactly leading the scoring race at the time, he was still something to see.

"You keep waiting to see him take his next shift," said WHA executive director Ron Ryan, after his first glimpses of The Boy Wonder. "You sit there and you can't wait for his next shift."

"People were still saying he couldn't skate and they were still saying his shot was nothing special and that he certainly didn't have the aggressive qualities of, say, a Bobby Clarke. "But," protested Inkpen, "he sucks you in when you think you've got him cornered."

"He passes the puck better than anybody in hockey," said veteran netminder Gary Smith.

"He has an extra sense," said Stapleton. "And he challenges defencemen. He has the ability to avoid traffic. He's so deceptive. A pure goal scorer would have a field-day playing with him."

Stapleton admitted he was a little bit leery of The Kid competing with grown men and, as a result, wasn't pushing Gretzky. "I didn't want to get him run down physically or mentally. I knew he'd been compared to Bobby Orr coming out of junior. But there's only one Bobby Orr. Wayne has a great hockey sense, but you've got to have patience. He's not going to be a star overnight."

Oh well...Even the people who believed in Gretzky occasionally underestimated his magic.

But there was nothing to misjudge in his character. What you saw was what you got.

"All summer long people kept asking me if I'd met Wayne Gretzky yet," said Indianapolis netminder Eddie Mio back then. "They knew I'd be playing with him and there'd been so much hoopla about his signing for so much money. It was all I heard. Gretzky! Gretzky! Gretzky! Well, then I met him. And talked with him. And I liked him! I realized, as did everybody else, I guess, that all the talk was not his fault. He's sure got the talent and I guess he was paid more for his potential at this point. He's a real personable and likeable kid."

Mio was going to spend more time around Gretzky. But not in Indianapolis.

Welcome to pro hockey, kid

In a classic case of *deja vu,* The Kid made it back to the same Edmonton Industrial Airport where Skalbania had landed back in June to announce Gretzky's signing in the first place. Skalbania had decided that the only way to keep the Racers afloat was to unload Gretzky. So it was, "Welcome to pro hockey, kid. You'll be lacing your skates in Edmonton."

He came into Peter Pocklington's possession with Mio and forward Peter Driscoll, and the three flew to Edmonton on a chartered Lear Jet which cost the Oiler owner $7,900. Pocklington has not, to date, complained about the price. It would have been less than that, except that the pilot wanted another $2,500 to fly from the International Airport to the Industrial Airport. Since they were more than two hours late for a press conference in the Edmonton Inn, Mio signed coach Glen Sather's name to the bill for the extra leg of the flight and they landed a block from the hotel at the Industrial.

"Maybe Nelson should have left me here in June," said Gretzky, who admitted he was a little shocked at the news that he had been sold to the Oilers by Skalbania.

But it could have been the Jets in Winnipeg. And if Jets' owner Michael Gobuty had it to do over again...

"Crazy Nelson," said Gobuty of Skalbania. "Nelson wanted to play backgammon for Gretzky against one-third ownership of the Jets. It was the day before Nelson sold him to Edmonton.

"To my chagrin, I didn't agree to the backgammon game. I found out later that I could have beat him. Nelson, I discovered, really isn't that good a backgammon player."

From that day on, Gobuty would be a permanent fixture on Pocklington's Christmas card list.

"You know, I almost had him without knowing it back in the summer," said Pocklington. "Gretzky's lawyers in Toronto at the time happened to be my lawyers. I told them I'd love to bring this kid to Edmonton. They told me he was too young.

"But a few months later Birmingham Bulls' owner, John Bassett, was talking to Badali about him. The price was too high for Bassett but he told them to get hold of either Pocklington or Skalbania. He'd just been on the phone talking to Skalbania so he suggested Badali should phone him. If he'd been on the phone talking to me..."

When Pocklington's turn did come, the deal for Gretzky wasn't complicated.

"When Nelson sold the Oilers to me, the deal was I'd have to pay him a half million if the Oilers got into the NHL," he said. "I gave him $300,000 cash and we ripped up the agreement for the half million. It was that simple. That's my philosophy. Keep 'em simple. And keep 'em big.

"The whole thing took about five minutes on the phone to finish off. Nelson needed the money right away."

An interesting sidelight to the deal was that the player Indianapolis chose to replace Gretzky was another seventeen-year-old from the Edmonton satellite city of St. Albert. The kid's name was Mark Messier. He was eventually to become an Oiler and Gretzky's team-mate. Messier is only eight days older than Gretzky.

"I was looking for something like this to happen," said Gretzky, who would say nothing negative about Indianapolis.

"In Nelson's eyes, I think he feels he's doing me a favor. He said Edmonton was the best sports city in North America...so I guess we'll see. It's funny though. Here I am, only seventeen, with a three-year head start on most guys, and I've already been traded."

Gretzky wasn't sure about Edmonton right off. "It's a big change, but I'm going to try to meet some kids here. Hopefully, I'm going to go to night school in January, so I'll get to know people there. And I'm pretty sure there's a girl I knew in Sault Ste. Marie who's moved out here..."

CHAPTER 5

OF GRAMPS AND THE KID AND
THE END OF THE WAR

One of the first truly memorable "Gretzky Nights" in pro hockey was December 13, 1978, in Cincinnati, Ohio. And it will probably be unique forever in Gretzky's pro career. It was the night Wayne Gretzky was benched!

In his game story from Cincinnati, *Edmonton Journal* hockey writer Matheson wrote: "If he'd been in a classroom, Wayne Gretzky probably would have been ordered to write 'I Will Not Be Too Offensive' 500 times on a blackboard. He might even have got a detention."

But since the grade twelve student was playing hockey for a living now, Edmonton Oiler coach Glen Sather resorted to benching the Boy Wonder for the first period of the Oiler-Cincinnati game. Basically for "not helping out enough on defence."

Gretzky responded to the slap on the wrist by coming off the bench to score his first pro hat trick in the final forty minutes.

"He could have sulked," said Sather, who was slightly miffed at the kid's minus-six rating in the first four road-game losses of the trip. "But Wayne got mad instead ... the smoke was coming out of his ears."

"I think that game made Wayne Gretzky a hockey player," Sather said later. "That night he stuck it to me, and he carried us to the win."

For sure the soon-to-be-eighteen Gretzky was phenomenal in the final forty minutes of that game. He scored his thirteenth and fourteenth pro goals on plays from behind the net and finished off the three-goal game with a shotgun blast from forty feet out in the third.

Being benched had happened once to Gretzky in junior hockey. ''It happened in my last year at Sault Ste. Marie,'' said Wayne. ''I can't remember who we were playing, but I think I got seven points, four of them goals, in the last two periods.''

Leduc No. 1 had nothing on Gretzky

By the end of December, they weren't calling him ''Brinks'' anymore. He was being called The Great Gretzky in Edmonton and while doubts existed throughout the hockey world, especially in NHL circles, Edmonton was convinced.

He'd only been an Edmonton Oiler for one month and twenty-six days. A mere blink of an eye, perhaps. But it was one percent of his life.

And there was no denying The Kid. He was the most exciting thing to happen to Edmonton since oil was discovered at Leduc No. 1 and Jackie Parker led the Eskimos to three straight Canadian Football League championships in the mid-'50s. Every hockey fan in town was convinced he was watching ''A Star Is Born.'' He took fairly ordinary hockey games and turned them into experiences. He took the puck and did things with it that defied the fan to remain unmoved. For six seasons in the WHA the Oilers hadn't really been worth paying to see. But for the last month and twenty-six days, Wayne Gretzky alone was worth the price of admission and then some. On December twenty-eighth he was only one point out of the WHA's ''top 10'' in scoring and that was already being recognized as a miracle. Especially considering the weights Sather had tied to his wings.

But he continued to soar. And so did his point totals.

Goaltender Dave Dryden spoke volumes on the subject of Gretzky after a game one night. ''Personality-wise, he's incredibly mature. He's thoughtful. He's not the least bit spoiled. And the thing I like best is that he's not self-satisfied. He stays out late after practice. He wants to be as good as he possibly can be. And he's not a follower. He's a leader.

''Talent-wise, his biggest asset is his ability to control the puck and himself. He has the rare ability to wait for somebody to make a little mistake and take advantage of it for everything it's worth. Most players have preconceived notions of what they're going to do. I'm convinced he doesn't.''

By now every hockey man in the WHA and dozens of others had compared him to some hockey great or other.

But Dryden recognized his genius back then. ''Really, you can't compare him to anybody. He's unique.

''With his talent and with the personality he has shown us so far, the sky is the limit. I've seen a lot of guys with talent who didn't put it to use. But I'm convinced this is one kid who has all sorts of talent and is going to use it all.''

That talent has meant that Gretzky's life is one of what most people would describe as daily thrills. But a bigger thrill than he'd ever dreamed of was just around the corner. Wayne Gretzky was to start out the New Year in the kind of situation that would make a public relations man drool.

Howe about that

The Kid, who wouldn't turn eighteen for three more weeks, was to centre a line of Gordie Howe, who had turned fifty and had become a grandfather the year before, and Gordie's twenty-three-year-old son Mark, in the opener of a three-game series between the WHA All-Stars and Moscow Dynamo at the Edmonton Coliseum. The youngest pro hockey player on the same line with the oldest. Number 9 and Number 99.

''I'll be on such a cloud for my first shift with Gordie, it'll be unreal,'' said Gretzky, who had been treated to what he claimed was the greatest day of his life when he met Gordie Howe in New York the previous summer. Howe had introduced him to singer Debby Boone, boxing great Muhammad Ali, and hockey's Bobby Hull, in that order.

''I'll be in a dream when they drop the puck,'' Gretzky grinned. ''I was happy just to be picked to play on the same team with Gordie, but on the same line! Me centering Gordie Howe! I think I might pass him the puck.''

When Father Time led The Kid out of the dressing room for that first game of 1979, you just knew the Old Man would have something to say. ''Gee, Wayne,'' the fifty-year-old said to the seventeen-year-old, ''I'm nervous.''

Wayne and Gordie Howe pose for this shot before the game
between WHA All-stars and Moscow Dynamo *(COLORFAST)*

Howe waited a moment for the reaction.

"He looked at me like I was crazy," giggled Gramps.

Howe, who had played in more all-star games than The Kid had played league games in his pro hockey career, began to laugh.

Moscow Dynamo failed to see the humor in the situation. Thirty-five seconds after the opening face-off, Gretzky scored his first goal.

To Gordie, this playing with a seventeen-year-old who looked like he way going to be a star, wasn't exactly a first.

There was this kid Mark Howe a few years back. But Howe was only forty-five back then. And Wayne Gretzky was only twelve.

While it took a little local press pressure to convince the WHA mental giants the Howe-Gretzky-Howe line was a natural, to say it was a success would qualify as "Understatement of the Year" material. The fans were so captivated by the line, they cheered everytime the trio skated on to the ice. It was a scrumptious scene.

Gretzky tries to be cool as "The Fonz" most times, but this was not a night for cool. The Kid, who already had enough thrills to last a lifetime, was asked to rate it.

"Tops," he said, sounding like a young kid who had just played on the same line as his idol, the greatest player in the history of the game, and scored two goals and added an assist against the Russians to be named "Player of the Game."

Even Old Number Nine was turned on by the situation. He played one of his best games of the season. Gramps was feeling young again. Frisky, even. "This is what keeps me going," said Howe. "It's fun!"

Then he complained that there was no beer in the dressing room. Such was the price of playing with a centre who wasn't old enough to have a beer.

"What's it like playing with your son and Gretzky?" he was asked.

"We were still the oldest line on the ice," chuckled Howe.

Howe delighted in retelling the stories about all the times he had met Gretzky. "I sort of took him under my wing in New York at the meetings this year," said Howe. "We had a super day. He met Debby Boone and he really got a charge out of that. I told him he must be a *real* rookie, because he didn't even ask her out. We met Muhammad Ali and Bobby Hull and he told me 'I'll never forget this day'.

"He played with my son Murray in Toronto, and I was at a dinner with him once."

"I was ten years old," said Gretzky. "I didn't know what to say, but Gordie helped me out."

"I dropped the puck to him at a bantam tournament once," recalled Gordie.

"I can't remember that," said Gretzky. "But if Mr. Howe said he did, then he did."

Gretzky said he's not sure if he'll believe, even twenty years from now, that as a seventeen-year-old, he played on the same line as fifty-year-old Gordie Howe.

"He's an amazing man," said The Kid.

"He'll never make it," said Howe with a giant grin.

January, 1979, was a month to remember. Not just because of Howe. Gretzky's birthday was coming. And The Kid was growing up a mile a minute.

Line-mates Wayne, Gordie and Mark Howe (*COLORFAST*)

Left red-faced by a 'movie star'!

The day before he turned eighteen, his team-mates had a little fun with him. For starters, the Oiler players jumped the gun a bit by buying a store-bought cake for him. And then shoved it in his face while a newspaper photographer snapped pictures.

There was one other comedy routine. At practice, Steve Carlson, who had a part in the movie "Slapshot," did his imitation of Gretzky the night before against the New England Whalers.

"It was hilarious," remembers former Oiler public relations director John Short, who caught the act. "They really stuck the needle in pretty good to dramatize Gretzky's act against the Whalers."

What had happened in the game was that Gretzky had been nailed by Gordie Roberts with a bone-jarring check. Gretzky hit the ice and threw his stick and one glove, in a temper tantrum.

"Carlson copied him to the hilt. He almost went so far as to take one of his skates off and throw it."

The red-faced Gretzky watched from the corner.

The Oilers may have been laughing at The Kid and making a point for his benefit (it was his final temper tantrum) in workouts. But they were at a loss for words to describe him in games.

Before his eighteenth birthday Gretzky had exceeded everybody's wildest predictions. He had twenty-three goals and forty-six points in thirty-nine games and was handily leading the Oilers in scoring.

"I remember him telling me he'd be happy with twenty goals and forty assists before the season started," said agent Badali. "The last time I talked to him he thought he might score fifty."

"I'd like to approach Mark Napier's total for an underage player," said Gretzky of another Badali client who fired forty-three goals as a nineteen-year-old with the WHA Toronto Toros in 1975-76.

"On the whole, my biggest adjustment has been realizing that pro goalies are quick learners. You can't beat them with the same moves you used in junior."

Junior. He still had two and a half years of junior eligibility remaining when he said that. And he kept getting reminded of his age.

"I can hardly wait for my birthday," he said often. "I'm tired of reading 'seventeen-year-old Wayne Gretzky' all the time."

One day he went into the lounge at the Edmonton Coliseum after practice with his team-mates. They ordered beer. He had a ginger ale. Gretzky was kicked out. He was too young to be there under Alberta liquor laws. The lounge manager, embarrassed at having to ask the rink's biggest drawing card and the Number One bringer of business to leave, offered to buy Gretzky a drink on his eighteenth birthday. Gretzky said okay, and he even came back and accepted the drink. He took a sip, made one of those faces a kid makes when he's forced to eat his liver, and offered the rest of the drink to someone else at the table.

Scenes like that made it all hard enough to believe. But when you considered that back home in Brantford, Wayne's parents were still collecting family allowance cheques for The Kid . . .

And what did you get for YOUR birthday?

On January 26, 1978, Wayne Gretzky turned eighteen. And there may never be a birthday quite like it in sport.

You've heard of a 99-year-lease? That's about what Edmonton Oilers had on Number 99 as of 8:09 P.M. on that historic date.

There was a cake in the shape of Number 99. A bottle of sparkling "baby" champagne from his team-mates. And the Oilers made it a surprise party for Wayne by flying in his parents, three brothers and his sister.

The birthday party was advertised.

But what came next wasn't.

Pocklington and the Oilers absolutely shocked the 12,321 fans by signing Gretzky, at centre ice, to a twenty-one-year contract. It would keep Gretzky an Oiler until 1999, if all the options were picked up.

How much? It was hard to say. But obviously, it made him a multi-millionaire.

Wayne signs the contract which will employ him as an Oiler until 1999 *(COLORFAST)*

"There's a negotiation clause after ten years," said Pockling-ton. "But there's no out," he quickly added.

"No out," admitted Badali.

"In the tenth year we will sit down and renegotiate because of all the factors such as inflation," said Pocklington. "If we can't agree, an arbitrator will be brought in."

Pocklington swore, that night, that he would not give up Gretzky as a price of merger and Edmonton fans weren't going to let him forget that promise. They wanted into the NHL. But not THAT badly, they didn't.

In many ways, though, as was the case in Skalbania signing Gretzky in the first place, merger was one of the inspirations for the deal.

"We tried to get the rights to the rest of the kids," said Pocklington of the three Gretzky boys, all of whom wore Oiler sweaters with 99 sewn on the back. One of them, eleven-year-old Keith, already had more than 100 goals that season.

"Maybe I'll play with him in six years," said Gretzky, quickly subtracting from seventeen.

That the contract should expire in 1999 wasn't settled until mid-afternoon that day. And according to all, it was more Gretzky's idea than anybody's.

"Gus tried to slow the deal down a little," said the then-Oilers' general manager Larry Gordon. "But Gretzky said he'd seen enough of Edmonton to know this is where he wants to play hockey for the rest of his career."

And there was one other thing. Number 99 liked the ring of 1999.

"Looks like I'm here for life," said Gretzky. "I've played in four different cities in the last three years. I don't need to go move again. Everything is great here. There's no sense to leaving."

For those still looking to see if matters would go to his head, there was little evidence of it. "There's more pressure on me now than ever before," he said in the dressing room after the game that night. "With this contract, I know I'm going to have to go out and earn it."

For the first twenty minutes of the deal it looked as if Pocklington had made a horrendous mistake. Gretzky couldn't have played worse. "I was so uptight I couldn't make a pass," said Wayne. "Heck I could barely write my name on the contract."

More uptight than he was playing on the same line with Gordie Howe in the first game of the WHA All-Star Series with the Soviets?

"I had Gordie Howe to settle me down in that game," The Kid quipped. "I didn't have him tonight."

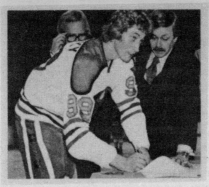

Former GM Larry Gordon and Oiler owner Peter Pocklington look on (*COLORFAST*)

How good is he, Bobby?

In the weeks that followed everybody in hockey was being sought out for an opinion of Gretzky. Was he going to be the "Next Bobby Orr," as the Oilers were obviously gambling?

In New York, at the NHL Challenge Cup Series with the Soviets, they were even asking Bobby Orr.

"He's good," said Orr. "I watched him in junior and I've heard so much about him that I know he's good. The puck just follows him around."

Orr talked of what it must be like for Gretzky. "I remember the first couple of years. When I was eighteen years old, all I wanted to do was play. I didn't think about anything else. I don't think he's thinking about anything else.

"If he is, consider it advice. You can't get worried reading this and reading that. Enthusiasm is a great thing."

The key, Orr suggested, was having the head to go with the talent. "I'm sure he's so talented he could get by at half speed. But you have to be enthused. You have to play 100 percent all the time. I wanted to play and I loved to play."

Orr was asked how a player in Gretzky's boots should handle the press at that age. Not that it was a problem. Gretzky was doing just fine in that department. But when the question was popped, a couple of veteran NHL reporters, eavesdropping on the conversation, started to laugh. "I never talked to them," he said, motioning at the sportswriters. "I was wrong many times. But I'd sneak away.

"I didn't think about the press clippings," he said. "I wanted to play pro hockey. I'll never forget what a thrill it was when I was told I could check into the Madison Hotel. That was a very exciting day for me. Being told you could check into the Madison Hotel meant you had made the team."

"If he works hard, he'll be very, very successful."

Orr was asked if he had any advice to pass on to The Kid in Edmonton. He took one look at the knee which had ended his career. "First I'd tell him to look after the body."

Bobby Orr said there really wasn't much advice he could give. It's very simple. "Work hard," he said. "He's very, very talented. If he works hard, he'll be very, very successful."

Already in pro company, Gretzky WAS working hard and he WAS becoming very, very successful.

110 points and "Rookie of the Year"

With the Oilers about to play their sixty-second game of the season, he already had eighty points. In his last seventeen games, he had thirty-two points. Almost two points per game. He'd slipped into fifth place in the league scoring race.

"I had some goals when I turned pro," Gretzky was admitting to the press now. "Twenty goals and forty assists."

On April tenth, he scored goals 39, 40, and 41. And got his fifty-eighth assist. That gave him 99 points, and considering his sweater number, it might have been a nice total to end with. But he closed with 110 points, finishing third in the WHA scoring race and winning WHA "Rookie of the Year" honors. The Oilers had finished atop the WHA for the first time ever and they should have won it all. But they lost out in what was to be the final Avco Cup playoffs. While they reached the final, the Oilers were beaten by the Winnipeg Jets and, in a typically candid comment the following year as Oilers were struggling to make the playoffs, a big part of the Gretzky character shone through.

He'd long since proved he was an eighteen-year-old kid with a twenty-eight-year-old head on his shoulders.

And on this night in Chicago, Gretzky pointed to a naked finger on his right hand. "There should be an Avco Cup ring there," he said. "We had the better team. But we ended up losers. And that's been in the back of my mind ever since. We had the better team but we didn't win. This year we've got the best team of the ones in the race for the last few playoff spots. If we don't make the playoffs, we've wasted the year. If we don't make the playoffs, we'll go to camp in September and we'll more or less be starting from scratch all over again. The whole thing about this year, because we're young and we're in our first year in the NHL, is to gain experience. To develop character as a team. If we don't make the playoffs, we'll go to camp and we'll be starting all over again."

But that was a year ahead of time.

Edmonton and the three other WHA teams had just been accepted into the NHL. And it was another sporting thrill for a city that used to be something of a pimple on the prairie, and was now experiencing what it was like to be big league. Gretzky was a big part of that. But not the only part.

CHAPTER 6

GRETZKY TACKLES THE NHL MYSTIQUE

The 1978 Commonwealth Games were a tremendous success, the Edmonton Eskimos won the Grey Cup, the Oilers made it into the National Hockey League, and owner Pocklington had purchased the Oakland Stompers of the North American Soccer League to bring to the city under the name of the Edmonton Drillers — things were happening on all fronts. Gretzky's faith in the city, as shown by his willingness to sign a twenty-one-year contract, wasn't without justification.

In the month the Oilers put their season tickets on sale, competition for the sports dollar was fierce. The Eskimos were in the middle of their annual season-ticket drive. The Drillers, who showed up in town a month before they were to play their first game, were also selling season tickets. The Oilers and Eskimos sold out in a flash. And the Drillers did surprisingly well considering the circumstances. In one month, more than $10 million of season-ticket business was done in Edmonton.

But NHL talk was dominating the coffee breaks. And the biggest discussion was how Wayne Gretzky would do under the Big Top. Nor was it restricted to Edmonton coffee shops. There was the same sort of talk in the other twenty NHL cities. "He won't do much next year. The checking is tighter in the NHL. They'll hit him. He'll be lucky to score twenty." That's what they were saying.

Gretzky heard the talk. And he wasn't buying it. "This is my fourth year as a 'rookie'," said the one and only individual player who was a factor in merger.

"Each year I've had to prove myself. Each year they told me the checking would be tighter. Each year they told me I'd get hit more. Each year they told me I wouldn't score. Every year I've been told I'm going to get run out of the rink.

"Next year will be my fifth year as a 'rookie'. I'll be going into the NHL at eighteen, just like Bobby Orr and Gordie Howe. There's going to be a lot of pressure. But I plan to prove myself next year too."

When owner Pocklington heard that he smiled. "It's going to be fun growing up with Gretzky. As he gets older, I'm going to get younger."

With Peter Pocklington acting like a proud papa, and all of Edmonton like a city of 600,000 adopted relatives, there was still the matter of returning to the real hometown — the real family and old friends — in Brantford.

Old friends wondered if he'd still talk to them

What was it like in Brantford after that marvelous first season in pro hockey and with a twenty-one-year contract with the Edmonton Oilers — the *National Hockey League* Edmonton Oilers — in his back pocket?

"It was a little weird," remembered Gretzky, who had returned to Edmonton in September as the same kid he was when he left — except his acne condition was a little better now.

"The phone never stopped ringing. And there were a lot of people who wanted autographs and stuff. But the people I used to know reacted a bit different too. I'd walk down the street and see people I knew and they'd be a bit edgy. I think they wondered if I'd still talk to them or something dumb like that. That's a funny feeling. But it didn't take long for me to convince them I hadn't changed much."

And he hadn't.

There were to be some changes in his lifestyle. But not many.

"I was thinking of going out and looking for an apartment," he said. "But I don't know. A lot of guys my age are still boarding while they play junior hockey. There's nothing wrong with it. I think I'll take my time and see what happens."

To be eighteen and not have to go to rookie camp

While it was "Back to Camp" for most hockey players, it was more than that for Gretzky. It was also "Back to School" like it was for most kids his age.

Ross Sheppard Composite High School.

And he wasn't planning to go incognito. "I don't think I'll be wearing a mask or growing a moustache or anything like that," chuckled Gretzky. It wasn't to be for long. He only had two credits to go to get his high school diploma. With his next twenty-one years covered by contract, Gretzky certainly didn't need school to make a living.

"Why?" seemed like a logical question.

"I promised my parents that I'd complete grade twelve," he said. "I also think going to school will keep my mind thinking. Keep me sharper. And it'll give me something to do on road trips. You can't read *The Hockey News* all day. I need Canadian history and English. My classes are in the afternoon. We practice in the morning. With two classes I should have no problems with road trips."

Meanwhile, the strangest sight at training camp was Gretzky, sitting in the stands, watching rookie camp.

"It's a funny feeling when you're eighteen and you don't have to attend rookie camp," he said. "Everybody there is older than I am."

"Hoo boy — I can't believe this is happening."

In pre-season, Gretzky picked up where he'd left off. And after one look, people like Phil Esposito of the New York Rangers were willing to admit everything they had heard about the kid had to be true. Gretzky scored five points in twenty-one minutes against the Rangers and in the post-game dressing room Esposito said, "He's the greatest young player I've seen since Bobby Orr."

The Oilers played their first National Hockey League game in Chicago. And all eyes, of course, were on Gretzky.

It was two hours before game time and in the bowels of Chicago Stadium, Edmonton Oilers were not only getting themselves up for the game, they were getting up-tight and out of sight.

"Hoo boy," said Wayne Gretzky. "I can't believe this is happening."

Before the game he was featured in both Chicago major daily newspapers and one front sports page interview carried the now usual "Great Gretzky" headline.

"When they play the national anthems, I know I'm going to get butterflies," he sighed.

Butterflies, however, are wee things. After the historic first Oiler game in the NHL was over, Gretzky and virtually all the Oilers admitted the things fluttering in their stomachs had a considerably larger wing span.

"I've never been that nervous before a game in my life," The Kid said, even counting the night he had played with Howe in the WHA all-star game and the night he'd signed the twenty-one-year deal.

Mark Messier, Oilers' other eighteen-year-old, said if Gretzky was nervous, he was petrified. "It really hit me in the afternoon," said Messier. "I sat in my hotel room and all I could think about was 'Hey, we're in the NHL.' It got to me."

It got to all the Oilers. They were an early disaster. People back in Edmonton, watching on television, had to be thinking for the first few minutes of the game that it was going to be a long year. Or decade. But the Oilers overcame their nerves to some extent, and nearly came back to win.

Rookie Kevin Lowe scored the first Oiler goal in NHL history with Gretzky drawing an assist. Gretzky was named the third star of the game.

Wayne and Kevin Lowe — the 'Odd Couple'

Lowe also settled Gretzky's quandary over whether to remain on room-and-board or get an apartment. The apartment won.

We take you now to a modest four-storey walk-up on Edmonton's South Side where we look in on Felix Lowe and Oscar Gretzky. "I wouldn't say Gretz is a terrible cook," says Lowe, the captain of the Quebec Remparts the year before, and Oilers' first pick in the NHL draft. "It's just that I'm a better cook than he is.

"And I don't know if I should be saying it," he added, "but

Gretz isn't doing too much homework so far. I'm going to have to get on him about that.''

The two worked out a deal with a fourteen-year-old girl of the family across the hall. She vacuums the apartment in exchange for hockey tickets.

Gretzky was in awe of Lowe's cooking.

"He's amazing," The Kid said. "Kevin cooks roasts, makes fondues and bakes lasagna. One night he even had a huge cherry cheesecake for dessert."

"I can't be that good," said Lowe. "I can't get him fattened up."

It was a great scene with those two kids the first few weeks. They were still young enough to talk about being thrilled without feeling as if it was unprofessional, or uncool.

"It's twice as much as I thought it would be," said Lowe of the NHL experience. "The excitement and glamor is incredible. In junior hockey I was a pretty popular person. But in pro, it's already way above that. It's more than I thought it would be. A lot more."

Lowe said he was delighted to be living with Gretzky because he felt some of the good things about his roomie were rubbing off on him. "At least, I hope so," he said. "He's unaffected. A lot of guys would have blown the situation Gretz is in. He's younger than I am. But it doesn't feel that way. We're getting on great as roomies. And he really isn't THAT bad a cook.

"We think a lot alike. We're both shooting for the same sort of thing. I know I'm not going to be content just being a fringe Oiler. I want to be a star. Gretz is a star already. But he wants to be the calibre of somebody like Guy Lafleur. I think we're both the kind of guys who are going to work every night to try to be as good as we can possibly become."

They're the Odd Couple all right. Odd in that it was amazing to find a couple of kids with their heads screwed on straight living under the same roof. So many young, suddenly-rich pro hockey players react badly to adulation and money.

By now Wayne Gretzky couldn't find a place in Edmonton where he wouldn't be recognized. But it wasn't turning him into a recluse.

"I still find it kind of neat to walk down the street and have someone know who I am and to want my autograph," he said. "I guess I take a bit of pride in that because it means I've done something people like."

On the subject of autographs . . .

"I don't mind the autograph hunters because I can remember my mother and one of her friends chasing after Bobby Hull to get his autograph for me when I was seven," he'd said.

But odd as it may have seemed for an eighteen-year-old who had written as much history as Gretzky, Edmonton was already starting to take him a little for granted.

Somehow, it seemed, he'd been thrilling Edmonton fans forever when he stepped on the ice against the New York Islanders on November 2nd. One year ago to the day, Wayne Gretzky had played his first game as an Edmonton Oiler.

A big win for the Oilers and 'first star' for Gretzky

The scene that night might be forever etched in the minds of the 15,418 who were there to watch the Oilers stun the Islanders 7-5. With thirty seconds to go, the fans were standing, hooting, and howling. But the crowd response to remember was when Gretzky was announced as the first star of the game. It wasn't a continuation of the din. It was more a polite, appreciative response. It was as if the crowd was saying "of course."

The Kid put on his greatest show in the NHL to that point. And it wasn't the two goals and an assist. Gretzky watchers were virtually unanimous about it. They'd never seen The Kid play better. And it was his first game back after missing a game and three-quarters because of tonsillitis. If his line-mates had hit the net half the times he set them up, Gretzky would have had half a dozen points, easy.

"Gretzky made me look like a donkey," summarized Islander goaltender Glenn "Chico" Resch.

Oiler coach Sather said Gretzky's first shift in the game said it all about The Kid. "The Islanders scored in the second minute of the game and their goal was Gretzky's fault. His mistake. And he knew it. He looked at me on the bench and I knew by his expression he knew it. He wanted to get out there

Gretzky attracts a lot of attention wherever he goes *(BRIAN GAVRILOFF, EDMONTON JOURNAL)*

and get it back right then and there. That's why he shot like he did.''

Gretzky came back and scored on the Oilers' first shot on goal twenty-one seconds later. ''That's the hardest shot I've ever taken in my life,'' said Gretzky. But then he showed his Gordie Howe-like ability to downgrade himself. ''To be honest, I was shooting for the other side of the net.''

Gretzky had four goals and nine assists at this point.

''Things just happen when he's out there,'' said line-mate Blair MacDonald, who wasn't ashamed to admit much of his success was due to Gretzky's playmaking. ''It's unbelievable how much he's matured as a playmaker. Last year he'd often just get to the blueline and shoot. But he learns fast. Now he gets to the blueline and waits for his three or four options.''

''I'll tell you one thing,'' said Sather on Gretzky's first anniversary as an Oiler. ''I wouldn't trade him for four New York Rangers AND Barry Beck. Oops! You know what I just did? I just compared him to somebody. That's the first time I ever compared Wayne Gretzky to anybody. I promised him when he came here that I wouldn't put any pressure on him by doing that.''

But by this point he'd been compared in some way or another to just about every great who ever played the game.

The NHL scoring race — ''You mean beat Jesus and God?''

On January 24, in preparing to play a game against the Toronto Maple Leafs on the first anniversary of his signing the twenty-one-year deal at centre ice in the Edmonton Coliseum, Gretzky made what would prove to be an interesting statement.

Asked if he thought he'd win the NHL scoring championship, he looked appalled. ''You mean, beat Jesus and God?'' he said.

Marcel Dionne and Guy Lafleur, he was willing to concede, were better than he was.

But the rest of the best in the NHL?

''I'm as good as they are,'' The Kid had decided. ''The key is to keep telling myself that I'm as good as they are.''

The night before, with nineteen seconds remaining, Gretzky

scored his fifth winning goal of the season. It was his first winner at home in the NHL. The other four were on the road. That number was significant in that it was the exact number of wins the Oilers had on the road.

Wayne is squeezed between Bob Murray and Tony 'O' Esposito in a game with the Chicago Black Hawks (*BRIAN GAVRILOFF, EDMONTON JOURNAL*)

Gunning for third but look out above!

With an assist earlier in the game against the Los Angeles Kings, Gretzky had moved into a tie with Charlie Simmer for fourth place in the NHL scoring race. And he was only three points behind third-place Dave Taylor. Edmonton had thirteen wins, and another revealing statistic was that Gretzky had thirty-two points in those wins. With twenty-six goals and forty-three assists, he was ahead of the pace from the year before when he scored forty-six goals and 110 points in the WHA.

You remember that league, the WHA, variously known in NHL circles as the Wishful Hockey Association, the Won't Hit Association, and the World Home for the Aged. A league which was supposed to be so inferior because it had a fifty-one-year-old man playing in it?

Gretzky at this point had 176 points in 125 games as a pro and he still had 112 games to play before he would have used up all his junior hockey eligibility.

Well, maybe, just maybe, all those people who said he'd be nothing special in the NHL were all wrong, hmmm?

"At the start of the season there were a lot of people who were still saying I couldn't play in the NHL," said Gretzky, opening a subject he hadn't dealt with since prior to the season — when he'd calmly predicted he'd prove them wrong, just as he'd done the year before in the WHA.

Gretzky was admitting now that he had set a goal for himself early in the season. He said he'd made up his mind that he wanted to finish third in the NHL scoring race.

He set that goal, he said, about two hours before game time one night in Maple Leaf Gardens after reading a program article about himself.

"It was all about what a good year I had last year in the World Hockey Association and it was really complimentary and everything. It predicted I'd probably do okay in the NHL but the last line of the article said I'd finished third in scoring in the WHA last year, but of course, there was no way I'd finish third in the NHL this year."

Once he drilled it through his head not to be in awe of the other stars, "Jesus" and "God" excepted, Gretzky figured he was on his way.

"Three years ago I was in the stands watching Gil Perreault and I was thinking he was the greatest. Now I have to go on the same ice with him and convince myself that I am as good as he is," said Gretzky, who admits he's been able to get up more for the games against the top players, when the challenge of proving himself by comparison was right there for all to see. Especially in their rinks. And Gretzky, at this point, had scored more goals on the road than he had at home.

"At lot of players get psyched out by all the talk. Like everybody tried to convince me that I'd really notice a difference in the hitting and checking in the NHL. I thought it would be tougher hockey than it is. I thought it would be more physical.

"A lot of players come into the NHL and get down on themselves. They get psyched out by just being in the NHL, by going on the road and by thinking all these guys are great."

The trophy they wouldn't allow him to win

But all those guys aren't Wayne Gretzkys. And by the All-Star break, Gretzky's accomplishments had reached the point where they'd already passed "remarkable" and "amazing" and had truly reached mind-boggling status.

And there began to stir a cry of "unfair" in Edmonton. A cry to make Wayne Gretzky eligible for the Calder Trophy as "Rookie of the Year" in the NHL. It was already becoming quite clear this young man was the best "first year" player in the NHL. Maybe the greatest "first year" player in history.

There was also quite the contradiction. The NHL wouldn't permit Gretzky "Rookie of the Year" status because he had one year of major league hockey in the WHA. And yet the NHL wouldn't count his WHA totals in the NHL record book because the WHA was a minor league.

Jim Coleman, nationally syndicated sports columnist of the Southam News Service, made the point:

> Up until the current season, the rules for awarding the Calder Trophy, as printed in the NHL's official guidebook, were: 'To the player selected as the most proficient in his first season of competition in the National Hockey League.' The rule also stipulated that 'the player cannot

have played more than twenty-five games in any single preceding season, not in six or more games in each of any two preceding seasons.'

Before the opening of the 1979-80 season, the rule was amended by the addition of the following five words: 'In any major professional league.'

As most fair-minded sports commentators across the country have been pointing out, the NHL amendment of its own rule appears to be aimed directly at Wayne Gretzky — although he hadn't even played his first NHL game when the change was made. Up until last summer's amalgamation, most of the NHL Big Domes scornfully had declined to admit that the WHA was a major league.

CHAPTER 7

THE OLD RECORDS FALL

As he headed for the NHL All-star game in Detroit, having just turned nineteen, Gretzky had thirty-two goals and fifty-two assists for eighty-four points. In his last nine games, Gretzky, who had registered his first three-goal game the week before against Winnipeg Jets, had nine goals and thirteen assists for twenty-two points. He was now only fifteen points behind Dionne and ten behind Lafleur. And people were beginning to think the "unthinkable" — that Gretzky could catch "Jesus and God."

With twenty-eight games to go, Gretzky had already passed Marcel Dionne's "first year" total of seventy-seven points.

Having scored eleven points in his last three games, this Wonderkid had also passed Richard Martin's "first year" total of seventy-four. And Bobby Smith's "first year" total, also seventy-four.

Gilbert Perreault, in his first year, had seventy-four points. Guy Lafleur had sixty-four. Seven more and Gretzky would tie Mike Bossy's "first year" total. And with twelve more he'd become the highest "first year" point producer in this history of the game, surpassing Bryan Trottier's ninety-five. There was no doubt he'd smash that record to smithereens. But he wasn't eligible for the Calder.

No argument — a place in history
There was one record, however, they couldn't do anything about. That came on the night of February 15 against the Washington Capitals. Gretzky took up official record residence

on page 136 of the NHL record book. His room-mate, record-wise, was Billy Taylor.

The Kid had seven assists in one game as he crushed Taylor's former employers 8-2. Taylor, who was suspended from pro hockey for twenty-two years in 1948 when a Detroit bookie implicated him in a gambling scandal, had held the old mark since March 16, 1947.

"Heck, that record is nothing," said Oilers' Dave Semenko. "He'll probably tie Darryl Sittler's record for ten points in a game too . . . but Gretz will do it in one period."

"I've been watching him since pee wee," said Washington coach Gary Green that night. "Nothing he does surprises me. He's smart as a whip and so quick. When he's playing a team that was as slow as we were . . . he just walks around us."

Gretzky, who had one five-point night and two four-pointers earlier in the season, was prepared for the big night. "I just had a feeling I might explode," he said. "Every time I passed the puck, somebody seemed to put it in."

Well, almost every time.

Al Hamilton, the only original Oiler from the first year in the WHA still with the club at the time, missed one late in the game. Gretzky had slipped Hamilton a perfect pass twenty feet in front of Capitals' netminder Wayne Stephenson but Hamilton's shot sailed wide.

"I blew it," said Hamilton. "If I'd scored, he would have been in the record book alone. But that's show biz."

"Tonight we just sat back and watched," whistled team-mate Dave Hunter. "Was this Gretzky's night or what?"

Well, yes. And no.

He'd actually brought down a couple of other records with the seven-assist performance.

On page 138 of the NHL record book were two other categories: a) Most assists, one game, by a player in his first NHL season. b) Most points, one game, by a player in his first NHL season. Note the wording: "first NHL season." It didn't say first rookie season and it didn't say first major league season.

But it would in the future. The scoop was that the NHL would CHANGE the wording! "We'll probably have to change it to read 'rookie' or 'first major league season','' said Ron Andrews, head of NHL statistics. "Gretzky is not eligible for either record.

"Mr. Gretzky has caused us some problems. Heck . . . It should be one way or the other. You can't very well say he's NOT a rookie on one hand and that he IS a rookie on the other.''

But the NHL was stuck with it. And Gretzky without.

"It would be nice to win that trophy,'' said Gretzky of the Calder that night. "I'd really be proud to win it. But they've ruled that I can't because I played in the WHA last year, so there isn't much I can do about it, is there?''

And the records for first-year NHL players which didn't count either?

"That's a little disappointing, too,'' said Gretzky.

But the night of the long faces, this wasn't.

Naturally, the first question in the dressing room was, "What did you have for breakfast?''

"Breakfast? Aw, nothing special.''

"You just blew one heck of an endorsement from Wheaties, kid,'' said a sportswriter.

"Hey, I'm still in a fog. Breakfast? Ya, it was Wheaties. Definitely, Wheaties!''

Agent Badali stood across the dressing room and shook his head as he faced an only slightly smaller media mob. Did he think Gretzky would turn out this good this soon?

"Why not?'' he answered. "He's been doing the same thing every year since he was eight. Besides, he has been due for a night like this.''

Actually, Badali said Wayne was just trying to show his twelve-year-old brother, Keith, which one of them is the first star of the family.

Keith Gretzky had been setting the Quebec City pee wee tournament on fire the same week. "In the first game they beat Sweden 5-4 and he scored four goals and had an assist,'' said Badali, who reported he already had THAT Gretzky locked up as a client, too.

"Listen, I wasn't going to take anything for granted. I asked last year just to make sure.''

"The kid is breaking my records down there," said Wayne, who came up with twenty-three points in the Quebec tournament in five games to destroy Guy Lafleur's record. "I guess I had to go out and get myself a record in case I lose that one to Keith."

Close-in action against the Whalers *(BRIAN GAVRILOFF, EDMONTON JOURNAL)*

Often, a double shift

Coach Sather used Gretzky to centre two lines enroute to the record. He took a regular shift on his own line of Blair MacDonald and Brett Callighen. And he also centered a make-shift line of Bobby Schmautz and Dave Semenko.

"I've heard a lot of people say that my endurance is bad, that my durability is bad," said Gretzky. "That's crap!

"I always took an extra shift in junior. I like extra work. I thrive on extra work. The more I play, the better I play."

Everybody was coming up with "He just never stops amazing you" quotes in the dressing room that night.

Like then team-mate Bobby Schmautz. "Wayne's just incredible. He's got great peripheral vision. The last time I saw a guy have a night like this was when Darryl Sittler picked up ten points against us when I was with Boston. Wayne picks up the puck as well on the backhand as anybody I've ever seen. He has a knack and the puck follows him around. Before he's done, he'll rewrite all the books. It's just too bad they don't consider him a rookie."

But Hamilton sort of said it all. "It's kinda fun to watch him, isn't it?"

The *Edmonton Journal*'s front page headline the next morning was: "HERE'S LOOKING AT YOU, KID!"

Barely was the ink of the headline dry when the paper in Gretzky's home town had its presses rolling with an editorial on the local boy-made-good, this from the *Brantford Expositor*:

> Hockey fans already knew it. But now the *Financial Post* has made it official: the greatest asset possessed by the Edmonton Oilers, now turning into one of the great money machines of professional sports, is a Brantford teenager named Wayne Gretzky. As the *Post* puts it: 'Gretzky is the crème de la ice crème. He is poised beyond his years, an incredibly gifted hockey player possessing more hockey sense than most NHL teams.' This is the sort of recognition Wayne Gretzky has been earning for some time now and which, along with his twenty-one-year contract worth about $5 million, is no

more than he deserves. But because of a narrow and inconsistent policy on the part of the National Hockey League, he is being denied one important form of recognition that is by rights, his. That is the Calder Trophy for the outstanding NHL rookie of the season. There is no doubt that he already owns it in terms of his achievements — more than 100 points in his first NHL season. Nobody in the history of the NHL has done that. But the NHL has decreed that because Gretzky played last year in the World Hockey Association, he cannot be considered as an NHL rookie. At the same time, of course, the NHL refuses to recognize his WHA statistics. This offends common sense and plain fairness. Oiler fans are protesting against this petty injustice. And we join with them, and with all the supporters of Wayne Gretzky, and fairness, in urging the small minds of the NHL to think again.

Oops! The Lady Byng candidate slips up

While the *Brantford Expositor* was fueling the fire lit months earlier in Edmonton, in regard to the Calder, by now people in Edmonton were starting to talk of Gretzky as maybe, just maybe, Hart Trophy and Lady Byng material.

That's why they all gasped on March 14.

Wayne Gretzky got in a fight! And against a local kid, at that. Edmonton product Doug Lecuyer and Gretzky went at it in the Coliseum in a game with the Chicago Black Hawks.

"It started earlier in the game when he took a dive in the first or second period," said Lecuyer. "I jokingly said he dives as well as he scores points. I started to take the body on him. Then we went behind the net and our sticks got a little high. I didn't expect Wayne to ever fight. He doesn't fight, does he?"

This night, he did.

Gretzky, who pointed out he once hung around the gym in Brantford with the Summerhays boys of Canadian boxing fame, raised his penalty total to nineteen minutes.

"The guys have been looking after me for years," The Kid explained. "It's time I looked after them. I can throw punches with both hands, too. But I couldn't get the left one free."

Gretzky's one experience as a goon was quickly forgotten even if it looked as though the fight might make the difference between Gretzky winning the Byng and not winning it. Guy Lafleur only had ten minutes in penalties. But when "The Flower" came to Edmonton, he wasn't talking about Gretzky the fighter.

'Mister' Lafleur

He was barely out of the shower after the Montreal Canadiens' game with the Oilers in the Coliseum two nights later when he was speaking of the just-turned-nineteen-year-old kid, who usually seemed all grown up but occasionally proved he wasn't.

"At the all-star game in Detroit, he came up to me and introduced himself," said Lafleur, shaking his head. "He called me MISTER Lafleur.

"And then he asked me for a couple autographs."

Gretzky, when confronted with the Lafleur vignette, seemed a trifle embarrassed. "Aw come on," said The Kid. "I have a lot of respect for Mr. Lafleur. But the autographs were for my kid brothers."

Gretzky was now ahead of Lafleur in the scoring race. But if he was to win, to beat Mr. Lafleur, Gretzky said it wouldn't be fair.

"You have to respect the fact that Mr. Lafleur was hurt for a while," said Gretzky, who with eight games to play had forty-two goals and seventy-four assists for 116 points. Lafleur — er, Mr. Lafleur — had forty-seven goals and sixty-six assists and 113 points. Mr. Lafleur missed six games. Gretzky, officially, had missed one. But he could only take a single shift in another game and he had played with tonsillitis most of the season which wasn't pointed out nearly often enough, perhaps because it just didn't seem possible that he was under a handicap with the accomplishments he'd managed so far.

"I don't think there's much more to say about Gretzky that hasn't been said," Lafleur stated. "He's a star!"

Lafleur said he didn't think it was any easier for Gretzky to get points than it was for him. "I think it will be tougher for him to get as many next year because they'll check him closer than they are this year. But I don't think it's any different in that way. And I don't think it's tougher to score when you're with a second-place team than an eighteenth-place team. It's just as hard.''

In the four games he'd watched Wayne against the Canadiens, Lafleur said, ''It seems to me he's working for the team. It seems to me that he's a team player and that's important.''

Gretzky on the subject of Lafleur: ''The best thing about him is that he's such a team man.''

Lafleur said he was delighted for Gretzky. ''The game needs another star,'' he said.

Earlier in the season Marcel Dionne said that in a couple years it would be Gretzky, not he and Lafleur, who owned the game. Lafleur agreed. ''I think he will. If he's lucky and avoids injuries, I think he will. I wish him no injuries.''

The Kid was saying, this night, that the most important thing to him was helping the Oilers to make the playoffs. But he was willing to admit that if one eye was on the standings, the other was on the scoring race. ''Let's be honest,'' said Gretzky. ''Who wouldn't want to beat Mr. Lafleur in the scoring race?''

''Wayne is a nice kid,'' countered a grinning Guy Lafleur. ''But I wish he wouldn't call me Mr. Lafleur. He makes me feel old already.''

Gretzky got his Lafleur autographs for his brothers.

And there was a lot of attention on the young Gretzkys — not just because their big brother was the story of the season in the National Hockey League.

''How do I tell him he can't be another Wayne Gretzky?''

Keith Gretzky, who was already being referred to as ''Wayne Gretzky all over again,'' made an appearance in *Sports Illustrated*'s ''Faces in the Crowd'' section. Keith looked like he'd score 100 goals for the third year in a row. The thirteen-year-old was earning his own headlines and so was eight-year-old brother Brent. When he went to play in a tournament in Kingston, Ont. the advertising for the event included the words ''featuring eight-year-old Brent Gretzky.'' Young Brent was already playing with older kids and he'd scored a bundle. He planned on moving up another division the following winter.

"Having Wayne for a brother puts extra pressure on the kids," Walter Gretzky explained. "But it puts the most pressure on young Glen. Everybody expects him to be the same as all the rest of the kids. It's been difficult for him."

Glen Gretzky was born with a club-foot.

"I think he realizes that we're just glad to see him out there and playing, but I don't know."

There had been emotional moments.

"The CBC sent someone over to interview us about Wayne for their show 'The Challengers'," said Mr. Gretzky. "We were talking about the kids. The interviewer asked me why Glen didn't start skating until he was six when the others were skating when they were two. I just said that he had a bit of a foot problem that held him back for a couple of years, that's all. The interviewer didn't ask anything more about it. But I happened to look across the room at Glen. The TV cameras didn't notice. But Glen had tears coming down his face."

Glen Gretzky not only had to have three separate operations to his foot, but he walks and skates with a pin through the bone.

"I thought none of the kids would top Wayne when it came to work," Mr. Gretzky continued. "Wayne would be out on the rink in the backyard when other kids were going to the movies. He was an incredibly hard worker. All the kids are hard workers. But Glen works even a little harder. I'll look out at the rink when the rest of the kids have gone in because it's too cold out. And he'll still be there, skating around those pylons."

Glen Gretzky, because of the pin in his foot, has to struggle to skate and has a great deal of trouble making turns.

"What's always bothered me is how do I tell him that he can't be like the others?" said his dad. "How do I tell him he can't be another Wayne Gretzky? But who knows," he said, "maybe he can be."

It was only house league hockey, but what Glen Gretzky had accomplished this year, said his dad, was something extra special. The biggest thrill of the year in the family was when Glen, not Wayne, made the all-star team.

"What he's done has been amazing," said Walter. "It's incredible."

Not that the Gretzkys weren't thrilled with Wayne. All of Brantford was. And Brantford didn't have any trouble figuring out how to honor its native son.

Brantford's "Athlete of the Year"

He'd been the biggest thing in the city of 69,000 since he was four feet tall and seventy-eight pounds in pee wee hockey. But until Friday, March 28, 1979, Wayne Gretzky had never been the "Athlete of the Year" in Brantford.

"Who won it before? Well, Gary Summerhays, the boxer, won it a lot of times," said Wayne when he was asked for a little background on the subject.

"I guess I've got about 100 awards over the years," added Wayne, who only weeks earlier was a unanimous choice as Edmonton's athlete of the year. "But this is a new one. My dad says I can have them all when I get married and have a house of my own. But he's gotta be kidding. They'd take up too much room."

Gretzky, though, wasn't in any way putting down the award or what the occasion meant to him. "It meant a lot,' he said. "And it meant just as much and more to my mom and dad. I mean, it's my home town."

The Oilers produced a chauffeur-driven limousine to carry Gretzky, Badali, Sather, and a few team-mates to Brantford for the affair which included a dinner, and a puck-dropping ceremony for an exhibition game between two junior B teams, comprised of many of Gretzky's childhood chums to commemorate the occasion.

The next night Wayne Gretzky would play his greatest game. It was a Hockey Night in Canada game and if there were any doubters left, this one quieted them.

Showcase night in Canada — removing all doubts

Two goals. Six points. He was simply a one-man show against the Toronto Maple Leafs that night. Spectacular! In his last eight games — seven of which the Oilers won to move back into the race for a playoff position — Gretzky had scored ten goals. A couple of nights earlier against Atlanta on the road, Gretzky had scored his forty-sixth and forty-seventh goals and set up the

(BRIAN GAVRILOFF, EDMONTON JOURNAL)

winner with 1:50 to play. Every night he'd contributed. Every night the story was virtually the same. Ron Low, a recent acquisition in goal from the Quebec Nordiques, would hold the Oilers in early and Gretzky would win it late. The two of them were working miracles. Ten goals in eight games for Gretzky down the stretch. And twenty-four points!

Prior to the arrival of Low, a certain *Edmonton Journal* sports columnist, who just happens to be the author of this publication, wrote that he'd eat his column, with sour grapes, sour cream, sauerkraut, and a twist of bitter lemon if the Oilers got into the playoffs. The sports columnist said the Oilers did not have enough leadership or enough character to make the playoffs. Low and Gretzky both supplied and brought out the missing ingredients. The Oilers were making a run at it.

And Gretzky was making a run at the scoring title.

In Brantford, the Gretzkys received "a record" thirty phone calls after the Hockey Night in Canada game from Brantford well-wishers. One of those calls came from the Ferris family of Brantford, who had taken a banner which received almost as much exposure as Gretzky during the telecast. The banner featured Marcel Dionne's total and Gretzky's changing total. Gretzky started the night with 127 points, six behind Dionne. He ended up with 133 and tied for the lead in the scoring race. Both the Oilers and the Los Angeles Kings, Gretzky and Dionne, had three games to play.

The night Gretzky had in Maple Leaf Gardens offered another insight into The Kid. Unquestionably the Toronto papers had provided Gretzky with more "ink" on a game day than he'd ever had in his life.

It brought back a conversation in the Oiler dressing room about a month earlier.

Kevin Lowe, the rookie who was rooming with Gretzky, had an interesting theory about Wayne. He said he could tell when Gretzky would have a great game on the road. All he had to do was wander down to the newsstand in the hotel, invest some change in the local dailies and check the space The Great Gretzky had received in the game-day editions.

"If they're writing reams about him, he'll score lots," observed Lowe.

Gretzky, a month before the Toronto game, admitted there was probably some truth to what Lowe said.

"It puts extra pressure on me," said Gretzky. "When the press is building me up, it promotes hockey and helps put people in the building. I guess I get out there and try especially hard to make sure I do as well as the press says I can do. Then, of course, there are the people who are coming to see me flop. And that's the other side of the coin."

With "Wayne Gretzky Day" in Brantford, all the publicity in Toronto, and a rare Oiler game on Hockey Night in Canada's national network, there was no lack of pressure. And when it was over, there was no lack of total, unrestrained, unreserved adulation for The Kid. Canada was, finally, sold on him.

But the question wasn't how Canada was taking all this — the question was, how was Marcel Dionne taking all this?

Dionne, after all, was on the cover of *Maclean*'s magazine. And it was obvious the cover story was intended to coincide with his finally winning the NHL scoring race.

"Only this past weekend," it said in the second paragraph of the *Maclean*'s piece, "with Dionne a distant sixteen points ahead of Montreal's Lafleur in the National Hockey League scoring race . . . the race seemed won."

There wasn't even a mention of Wayne Gretzky.

Dionne's a fan, too

Marcel Dionne had just returned from watching the Long Beach Grand Prix on the Sunday afternoon following Gretzky's heroics in Toronto, when he answered the long distance telephone call from Edmonton.

"I didn't see it, of course," Dionne said of the telecast. "But I've been talking to a few people who watched it on Hockey Night in Canada. I guess he was unbelievable, eh?

"I guess he showed EVERYBODY. If what he did Saturday night was like the reports I heard, I guess there won't be a person in Canada who isn't convinced what he can do now, eh?"

He laughed about Gretzky having referred to him and Lafleur as "Jesus and God." Marcel Dionne, for sure, was not sounding like a guy who was upset with the prospect of losing "his" scoring title to a nineteen-year-old kid.

"What he's doing this year is amazing," said Dionne. "I don't think anybody has seen anything like what he's done down the stretch for a team. They're going to be able to build the whole franchise around him. I'm convinced if Edmonton is smart with trades and drafts that they'll be a contender in no time. And someday, if they do that, and Gretzky remains healthy, Edmonton will win a Stanley Cup.

"If he wins the scoring title," said Dionne, with no hint of a challenge involved, "he'll deserve it. The Kid is great. He's unbelievable. I had a big lead, but he's come on. Make no mistake. He's nobody's fluke.

"I can't take anything away from that kid. He's going to have a lot of pressure on him in the future to be as good as he has been this year, but from everything I've heard of him, he thrives on that sort of thing. He has a great future ahead of him. It's great. For him. For your city. For the Oilers. And for hockey.

"Can you imagine him five or six years from now? As for records, he might break them all."

Maple Leafs' coach Joe Crozier said it best for Gretzky's game in Toronto. "Everybody came to watch Wayne," he said. "Including my team."

But if he excited all of Canada that night, the first visit to Maple Leaf Gardens earlier in the year was almost as big of a kick.

"It's a great thrill to play here," Gretzky said. "From the time I was two years old, I always wanted to play here."

But more thrilled than Wayne were both of his grand-mothers.

"I've waited a long time for this," said Mrs. Mary Gretzky of Canning as she waited for her grandson outside the Oilers' dressing room. "I always knew he'd play here, he was so good."

"She was just shaking," her son Walter recalled of the grandmother. Equally thrilled was Wayne's other grandmother Betty Hockin of Brantford as they watched The Kid score two and set up two others in a 4-4 tie.

"When I was six or seven, I used to spend every weekend at Grandma Gretzky's place in the country and we never missed a Saturday night game on TV," Wayne remembered after the game that night. "She liked Frank Mahovlich and I liked Gordie Howe. We used to have a thing going about that."

The Butler did it

A few days after the second Toronto game most of the hockey people who still possessed some sort of theory that Gretzky could be stopped and would be stopped the following year, may have been able to hold out some "hope" for the future.

They were all big games now, for the Oilers as a team, and for Gretzky in the scoring race. The next one was in Vancouver and the Canucks, too, were battling for a playoff berth with three games remaining.

And, when it was over, it could be said "The Butler did it!"

Stop Wayne Gretzky and you stop the Edmonton Oilers. That was the game plan for the Canucks. And it worked. Oh, how it worked!

Molson Breweries had spent $400 to set up a "clinch the playoff spot" party for the Oilers after the game in the Pacific Coliseum, but thanks to the checking job of Canuck winger Jerry Butler, the Canucks humiliated the uptight Oilers 5-0 and moved into a three-way tie with the Washington Capitals and the Oilers for the final two playoff spots.

Gretzky managed precisely one shot on goal all night — and that from the blueline — and only had the puck at his already-famous "launching pad" behind the net on two occasions.

Had somebody finally figured out how to stop Wayne Gretzky? Under the right circumstances, said Canuck coach Harry Neale, the answer is "Yes."

"You can't do it night after night," said Neale. "You have to get psyched for it. It's not as simple as checking a great goal scorer. What we're talking about here is stopping the best and most creative playmaker in the National Hockey League.

"But if you are the home team and you are willing to break up all your lines, you can do it."

It was only the seventeenth time all season that Gretzky did not get a point. The Oilers, for what it's worth, lost sixteen of those games. But nobody had shut him down like this before. Gretzky didn't get a sniff.

"The worst thing that happened to Edmonton was having their game against Toronto on national television," said Neale. "We watched the tape of that great game The Kid had, over and over and over again. And we made a tape out of the parts we wanted to use and brought Butler in and went over it with him."

Hockey not being nuclear physics, it's not the most complicated strategy ever devised.

"Butler's assignment was to stay with Gretzky regardless of where he went. As soon as Gretzky jumped over the boards, we hauled off the right winger and sent Butler over. The first thing we wanted to accomplish was for the Oilers to look up every time and see that Gretzky was covered. With Butler on Gretzky our defence didn't have to worry about Gretzky behind the net. But basically the idea wasn't so much to cover him as it was to force Gretzky to spend half the night trying to get away from Butler. We just wanted him to have to put in as frustrating a night as possible. We just wanted to take the three-point night away from him."

Butler admitted it wasn't easy. "I think I've a crick in my neck," he said in the Canuck dressing room. "I spent a lot of time trying to find him. But he better get used to it. With his play-making ability, he's going to get a lot of it."

"It worked tonight," said Neale. "But all the great ones manage to overcome it. And he sure as hell is a great one."

Gretzky wasn't held off the scoresheet for long. Only two games remained and the Minnesota North Stars, a team which had checked Gretzky with more success than most, were visitors in Edmonton.

Oilers only managed one goal in the game. But it was Gretzky who scored. Dave Hunter sent a forty-five-foot shot at the Minnesota goal and Gretzky rapped the puck into the net with his back to the goal. And it was a 1-1 tie. With Gretzky on the rampage, the Oilers had only the Vancouver loss in their last ten games.

"He hit it really solidly," said North Star netminder Gary

Edwards, who would later be an Oiler team-mate. "I didn't even know he was there and he timed it perfectly."

It was number 50 for Gretzky.

Gretzky put on a tremendous show. He had six shots and sent a half-dozen team-mates in on net with excellent opportunities they missed.

The season was summed up perfectly with the *Edmonton Journal* headline after the final game: "OILERS ARE PLAYOFF BOUND," was the overline, "ABOARD THE GRETZKY EXPRESS."

Edmonton beat Colorado 6-1. And Gretzky scored Number 51 and added two assists.

The Kid could hardly talk after the game because of the tonsillitis. He admitted he was weak. And he didn't think he played that well.

Neither did Bobby Schmautz, his former Oiler team-mate who was back with former Bruin coach Don Cherry in Colorado. "Even on the nights when he doesn't play real well," said Schmautz, a former team-mate of Bobby Orr, "he still gets three or four points. The great ones can do that. I can remember Orr getting two goals and two assists on nights when he wasn't on, too."

Would he be shut out at trophy time?

But it just wasn't Gretzky's year to win anything. Or, so it appeared. He didn't win the scoring race. The Art Ross Trophy was won, instead, by Dionne. Not because Dionne beat Gretzky in the scoring race — Wayne tied him. But Dionne had two more goals. And that gave him the trophy. Again, Gretzky had been deprived of an award by a technicality.

Jim Coleman, the dean of Canadian sportswriters, put it perfectly the next day in his nationally syndicated column for Southam News Services:

> Has it occurred to anyone that — if unforeseen circumstances forced Wayne Gretzky to retire from hockey right now — his name probably never would be seen engraved on a single NHL trophy for the edification of future generations of sportsminded Canadians?

God forbid that anything should happen to The Kid. But as far as the league's official memorabilia is concerned, what will he have as a lasting souvenir of the most gloriously exciting season which a nineteen-year-old ever has provided for Canadian hockey spectators?

The Art Ross scoring trophy was plucked from young Gretzky's outstretched fingers by Marcel Dionne, an equally deserving oldster.

The Calder Trophy, awarded annually to the oustanding rookie, has been legislated out of Gretzky's reach by the Big Domes of the NHL.

What's left for him? The Hart Trophy?

Probably he DESERVES the Hart Trophy, which is awarded annually to 'the player adjudged to be the most valuable to his team.' However, is he likely to receive the votes of the majority of news-media selectors from all twenty-one NHL cities, most of which lie within the borders of the United States?

What's left? The Lady Byng Trophy? Well, Wayne received only nineteen minutes in penalties but how about Guy Lafleur of Montreal, who has only ten minutes of penalty time?

Unquestionably this has been 'The Season of Wayne Gretzky' as far as the world of professional hockey is concerned. But it is a season from which sports' new Boy Wonder may emerge without a single piece of silverware to remind future generations of his prodigious feats in his NHL rookie year . . .

But the awards were out of Gretzky's hands. The ballots from hockey writers around the NHL were in the mail by now.

And nothing Wayne Gretzky could do in the playoffs . . .

Being there was everything in the first year
Ah, the playoffs!

Being there, of course, was everything for the Oilers in their first NHL season. "When you've been there, you know how to get there," Gretzky said. "And that's what this whole season was all about to me."

The Oilers were now winners, not losers. So easily could it have been the other way: going to training camp in September, and wondering if they knew how to win.

The Oilers, Gretzky said, would have that playoff experience to draw from for the next year. And they'd be a better team because of it.

"We won't be like Colorado and maybe Washington. They've never been there. We won't have to go through that," explained The Kid.

"This team will be playing in the Stanley Cup finals in three or four years," said Ron Low. "Any team with Wayne Gretzky on it, has to be. He's that good."

When the losers were winners

History would record a Philadelphia Flyers sweep over the Oilers. One. Two. Three. No runs. No hits. No errors. Nobody left on base. A first-place team wiping out a sixteenth-place team in straight games. History unfolding as it should.

But in this case, history would be full of beans.

Twice the Oilers took the Flyers into overtime, once in Philadelphia in the first game of the best-of-five series. And then, the third game, the Oilers took Philadelphia into DOUBLE overtime before losing on a goal by Bobby Clarke.

"They should be damn proud of themselves in that other dressing room," said Flyers' coach Pat Quinn of the team which had to win eight and tie one of their last eleven games to get into the playoffs on the last day of the season. "They showed us their mettle. They showed what they're made of and what they're going to do in the future."

Clarke said it really wasn't fair that the Oilers didn't win a game.

"Let's face it," he said. "The whole series could have gone either way. We could just as easily be down 2-1 today as series winners in three straight games. There's no way they'll be a sixteenth-place team next year. Not with this experience. Not with Low playing like that for them in goal. And certainly not with Wayne Gretzky and Mark Messier. They're both, obviously, outstanding. The only thing that beat them in this series was our experience."

A goal against the Hartford Whalers signalled by the now-famous patented Gretzky kick *(KEN ORR, EDMONTON JOURNAL)*

"Now they've got the experience of a playoff drive and a playoff series," said Bill Barber. "And of course, they've got Gretzky."

Ah, that's the rub. They've got Gretzky. And in certain Eastern Canadian precincts, the fact that Edmonton had The Great Gretzky instead of, say, Toronto, was a little annoying. Perhaps more than any other city in Canada, maybe even Edmonton included, Toronto had fallen head-over-heels in love with The Kid.

"If Gretzky were employed in New York or Toronto and were in this same position and doing all these wonderful things, he would be very big news indeed," wrote respected *Toronto Star* sports columnist Jim Proudfoot.

"Matter of fact, you wouldn't have read much else all season. He'd be in every magazine, in every newspaper, on every television show and on every billboard. He'd be making a fortune in commercial endorsements.

"But he's out in Edmonton. And he's virtually anonymous."

Well, if a westerner were tempted to tell a scribe from "Upper Canada" to go freeze in the dark...

Oilers' owner, Peter Pocklington, who had given Gretzky a new Porsche in lieu of the Calder, estimated Gretzky had been responsible for the destruction of an entire forest to produce the paper for the ink he'd received while playing in Edmonton.

"How much more ink can one player get? As for endorsements, you should see what The Kid has lined up for this summer. And as for Toronto... well, I'm totally confident that if we make the right moves in the off-season that we'll pass Toronto in the standings next year and leave them behind us forever. Five years from now, Toronto sportswriters can come to Edmonton to cover the Stanley Cup final."

"We're more than happy with the endorsements we're getting right now," said agent Gus Badali. "There are some excellent things happening, not just from a national point of view, but from a local point of view. We're not complaining. Edmonton has been good to us."

"We take the Toronto papers and all I know is that we read more about Wayne in the Toronto papers than we do about anybody else," said Walter Gretzky. "And as for the endorsements, that's ridiculous. He's got more than enough going for him. Heck, Gus is trying to find out when he can get him in the hospital to fix his tonsils. With his schedule this summer, it's tough to fit in a week and a half."

When the summer was over, it was quite obvious that Gretzky had done quite well in that area. The kid with the pimples had a couple of sweet deals endorsing a chocolate bar and a soft drink. The kid who hardly had enough whiskers to shave, had a razor endorsement. In addition to Neilson's Mr. Big chocolate bars and 7-Up, Gretzky had Bic Razors, GWG blue jeans, Titan, and Jofa.

What a summer Wayne Gretzky would experience. So busy, in fact, it was a fair question to ask him, when he arrived for camp in 1980-81, if he was coming to camp tired and worn out.

"I'm refreshed," he would say. "It's really been fun. I wouldn't do it if it wasn't. If it gets boring, I'll stop doing it. But I really enjoyed this summer. I'd rather be out doing things than sitting around doing nothing and wasting my time. That's the way I am."

He'd even sub for other hockey players at a moment's notice.

One day Mike Bossy got in a jam and was unable to be in Halifax to represent Titan hockey sticks at a sporting goods store. Gretzky jumped on a plane and replaced him. No problem.

"I wasn't doing anything that day," said Wayne, who worked more than twenty-five banquets during the summer.

The razor blades were good for a laugh.

Room-mate Kevin Lowe was telling the story at training camp. It seems he'd received a call from a shipping company saying they had some crates for Gretzky. He'd informed them they could deliver the crates. He couldn't believe it. Four giant crates of Bic razors.

"Yup, 4,000 razors," Gretzky smiled. "I guess I'll have enough of them left over for my grandchildren when they start shaving."

The endorsement offers were unbelievable.

Not only were there the ones previously mentioned. "I'd say

we turned another twenty down,'' said Wayne. ''We like to work with quality companies with good images.''

But he didn't spend the summer doing nothing but chase after the almighty dollar. In addition to working a Bill Heindl benefit game in Winnipeg, he worked with the Heart Foundation, the United Way, the Red Cross and was named honorary chairman for the Non-Smokers League. The appearances for charity took up more time than the business deals.

He appeared in Sault Ste. Marie to drop the puck to launch a new season and participated in a between periods ''Showdown'' competition. There was the filming of the Superstars competition. And there was even time for a little baseball.

While he declined an offer to try out for the Toronto Blue Jays farm system (saying, ''Is it true they only get $650.00 a month on the rookie league team in Medicine Hat?'') he managed to bat .492 with Brantford in the Intercounty League, knowing Oilers' owner Pocklington was sitting in Edmonton with his fingers crossed that Gretzky wouldn't get hurt.

''I'm not insured for this, you know,'' he told a reporter who came to watch him play what he still claimed to be his favorite sport. ''If I get hurt, when we're half way to the hospital, we've got to make it look like a car crash.''

Oh, and there was one other engagement Gretzky had to work in to his busy schedule in the summer. An awards ceremony in Montreal.

Despite the concern, Gretzky did just fine in the silverware department as well.

The King is retired; 'Long Live the King'

''BYNG-O!'' screamed the *Edmonton Journal* front page headline on June 5, ''THE KID HAS HART.''

It was a day like no other in hockey history. On the same day Number 9 officially retired from hockey, Number 99, The Great Gretzky officially ascended his throne.

It was only two years earlier that Howe met Gretzky at a World Hockey Association function in New York and now Wayne was telling the world that Gordie had given him some advice he planned to live up to for his entire career.

''Gordie just told me to give it everything I had every day to try to earn my money and to try to blot out the rest. If I did that he said, when I left the game, I'd be able to leave it without any regrets.''

Howe left the game without any regrets that day and Gretzky reaped his first rewards.

He was informed that day, by Peter Pocklington, that he'd won both the Hart Trophy as the Most Valuable Player in the League and the Lady Byng Trophy as the player best combining ability and sportsmanship. At nineteen, he was the youngest player to win either award. And only four times in the entire history of the NHL had one player been so honored with both awards in the same year, the most recent being Stan Mikita in 1968.

''I remember when I was in Montreal at the award ceremonies last year and I saw those trophies. There were a lot of people kidding me when I looked at them. But I made up my mind when I looked at the Hart, that someday I'd have my name on that one. I felt then, if I tried as hard as I could, I'd be able to do it. I've always thought that there's no use shooting for a medium goal. You have to shoot for the highest goal. And other than the Stanley Cup, that's the greatest trophy there is in the NHL.''

But to win it in his first year...

''When a fifteen or sixteen-year-old like Tracy Austin can win the world tennis championship,'' said The Kid, ''I didn't think it was impossible for an eighteen-year-old to win one of those trophies.''

But the really mind-boggling aspect of it all wasn't just somebody his age winning the Hart and the Lady Byng. It was the fact he should have also won the Calder and shared the Art Ross with Dionne.

This magnificent rookie could have won the ''Grand Slam.''

''I have mixed emotions about the other two trophies,'' admitted Gretzky, on the day he was told of the two he did win. ''I understand that when the Art Ross Trophy was awarded, it was stipulated by the Ross family that they wanted one winner. But when Bobby Hull and Andy Bathgate tied, the owners should have had a vote. I hear they are talking about splitting he trophy in the event of a tie in the future. And they should. I on't think it's right the way it is. I have younger brothers and hey have a lot of friends and they've all been brought up to elieve an assist is just as important as a goal. The kids are aving second thoughts about that now. The kids don't believe hat any more.

"As for the Calder, I was disappointed about that. But I have admit that I did know when I signed with the WHA, that it vould be that way. I can't blame anybody but myself and, to ome extent, the league because they didn't recognize the VHA a couple of seasons earlier."

And as for the Hart and the Lady Byng, Wayne Gretzky was aying, "One is just as nice as the other. Maybe someday we'll vin a Stanley Cup to put between the two."

Gretzky added that he felt he could not have been in the unning for the Hart without his team-mates.

"In those last eleven or twelve games all the guys played a ig part. We showed character at the end of the season and won en of the last twelve to get into the playoffs. If we hadn't made he playoffs, I wouldn't have won the award. I owe a lot to my eam-mates."

Mark Messier, a team-mate who is only eight days older than Gretzky, pointed out how it would be for him if he'd stayed in unior hockey for his final year of eligibility in 1980-81.

"Can you imagine Wayne playing junior hockey right now? would be a joke!"

With awards, of course, came concern. Having won them, he pressure − from now on − would be so intense it could round Superman much less a nineteen-year-old boy going on venty.

If it was bothering The Kid, it wasn't showing.

Maybe now, he'll be healthy

He said he was looking forward to the next season like no other because it'll be my first year in pro when I've been totally ealthy."

That's not a misprint. That's what he said.

A translation shouldn't be required but, if you needed one, was "Baby, you ain't seen nuthin' yet."

Everything about Wayne Gretzky is just a little bit unbelievable, but to think that he was playing at less than 10 percent...

Not much was made of Gretzky's tonsillitis during his first season in the WHA and his first season in the NHL. Oh, it was mentioned now and then, but never prominently. It sort of came off as being in the same ball park as a hang nail or hay fever. The Kid, certainly, didn't make much of it. And the writers didn't either. Let's face it. It was a tough story to sell. With Gretzky the most successful first-year player in the NHL history, it was a little difficult to convince people he was playing with a major handicap. It still is.

"People don't know how difficult it was for him," said Walter Gretzky. "There was a lot of poison going through his body. It was really bad at the end of the season. And before he went into the hospital, he tried to train for the Super Star competition and he couldn't even breathe. That's the size they were. We're so glad they're out and we're looking forward to this year because, believe it or not, as Wayne says, it really will be the first year since he turned pro that he'll be able to play 100 percent healthy."

Gretzky confessed, after the season and after he won the awards, the tonsillitis was much worse than he made out. "Over the past two years, the tonsils bothered me quite a bit. I didn't have the endurance and the stamina I should have had. I wasn't eating properly and I wasn't sleeping properly. I had to take penicillin during the whole season and use throat lozenges every game," said the nineteen-year-old, who had the tonsils removed at a small hospital in Paris, Ontario to avoid the maddening crowd of well-wishers he'd have had to face if he'd been in a Brantford hospital.

"My tonsils were bothering me so much, I saw four different doctors in Brantford and two in Edmonton. And it got worse and worse toward the end of the season. In the two years I've played pro hockey, my tonsils bothered me every game."

Coach Glen Sather said, "Everything he has done has led

me in total awe. And that includes what he accomplished despite the fact he was playing when he was sick. There were nights he should have been in bed. But that's what makes him so great. To him, being sick was just one more challenge.''

If there was pressure from the awards, Gretzky had just added more with the suggestion that in the season ahead his performance would not be hampered by illness.

CHAPTER 8

THE GREAT GRETZKY

It would, everyone agreed, be a tough act to follow. After winning the Hart Trophy and the Lady Byng, and ending up tied for the scoring title with Marcel Dionne at 137 points in your first season in the National Hockey League, what do you do for an encore?

"I thought about the 137 points and the awards over the summer," The Kid confessed when he showed up at his second NHL training camp.

"Maybe I put a knife to my own throat.

"I guess I've made it tough on myself. You know the old saying: 'If you score two goals, they want three.'"

Still, Gretzky hadn't changed his tune.

"I feel a lot stronger now that my tonsils are out. I'm really looking forward to this year. I think we have a lot better team now, and I have more desire to get going than I ever had. I still have a lot of things to prove. There are still a few doubters. I see, for example, that Marcel Dionne has changed his tune. He was quoted in *The Hockey News* as saying I 'won't have proved myself until I've been in the league for five years.'"

As a 19-going-on-20-year-old, Gretzky said his ambition was "to score one more goal than Marcel Dionne" this season.

Although some people were talking of Gretzky as a one-year-wonder, the majority were viewing him as a legitimate great now. And some were even asking him if he were the best player in the NHL.

"Guy Lafleur is the best player in the league," said Gretzky. "Someday I hope to be."

If he wasn't about to surpass Lafleur as the best player in the game in 1980-81, he was certainly about to close any gap there might have been between the two.

It becomes more difficult now to remember that Gretzky was only 19. For instance, when Oilers' media guide came out, 20-year-old rookie Glenn Anderson listed 19-year-old Gretzky as his "childhood idol."

Anti-Gretzky strategies?

The first question of the new 1980-81 season was, "What off-season adjustments had been made by the hockey minds to stop Gretzky in his second season?". Everybody had had a whole summer to think about stopping The Kid and surely anti-Gretzky strategies would have been developed.

When Gretzky scored only two goals in a ten-game stretch from late October to mid-November, there were some who believed the NHL brain trust was beginning to solve the Gretzky puzzle.

It was wishful thinking. Gretzky was off to his usual "slow" start. And he had a new winger, a chap by the name of Dave Semenko, for starters.

Now Dave Semenko was not renowned as a goal scorer. Or a playmaker. He was renowned as the Heavyweight Champion of the WHA. His old nickname was Dave Cement Co. His job, to this point, was more along the lines of winning fights, not scoring goals. And it was fair to say that a great many Edmonton hockey fans cringed when Semenko was sent on the ice to play hockey instead of fight.

If there ever was proof that you could put the Zamboni machine on Gretzky's wing and turn it into a goal scorer, this was the evidence. Or so a great many writers editorialized.

Former NHL bad-boy Bryan Watson was the Oilers' coach for openers that season and he was clearly enjoying the sudden success of Dave Semenko on the Gretzky-Blair MacDonald line.

"I guess you guys are using keys on your typewriters you've never used before," Watson said to the sportswriters. "I just love it," he said of the situation.

Semenko was actually blushing a bit. He fired seven goals in a six-game stretch playing with Gretzky.

"In the last minute of one game," said Watson, "there was an open net situation. Semenko looked at me and said, 'For crying out loud, coach, don't put me on the ice. If I score another goal, I'll have a hat trick and, if I do that, they'll expect another one next game.' "

Semenko and Gretzky were asked to stay out on the ice for the three-star selection in the game in question.

"When Dave came back into the dressing room, everybody was asking him, 'Which one were you?'. Semenko pulled his hand out of his glove and put up one finger, meaning first star, and he blushed."

Dave Semenko didn't last long on the line. Brett Callighen came back from an eye injury and replaced him. Bugsy Watson didn't last long as coach, either. General manager Glen Sather returned to dual duties. And MacDonald was traded to the Vancouver Canucks and a 20-year-old Finn, Jari Kurri, moved into the right-wing job.

Canada's Male Athlete of the Year

As the season progressed, any doubts about Gretzky being a one-year-wonder had disappeared.

And, in the annual Canadian Press year-end poll, Gretzky was named Canada's Male Athlete of 1980.

Gretzky — who had also won the Charlie Conacher Award which goes to the NHL player who makes an outstanding contribution to humanitarian or community service projects — was an overwhelming choice over Terry Puhl of Melville, Saskatchewan, an outfielder with the Houston Astros of baseball's National League.

Gretzky received 50 first-place votes, 32 seconds and 10 thirds. Based on a 3-2-1 evaluation, that gave him 224 points, Puhl received 11 firsts, 23 seconds and one third for 80 points. Canada's heroic one-legged runner Terry Fox of Vancouver placed third, golfer Dan Halldorson of Shilo, Manitoba, was fourth, and Dionne placed fifth.

Puhl didn't curse Gretzky for costing him the Athlete of the

Year title. He did, however, curse his luck one evening.

"I was in Edmonton one night when Winnipeg was playing there," he said. "I had to go to a banquet when I wanted to go to the hockey game. Wayne Gretzky scored three goals and had three assists that night. It would have been something to see."

And, unlike the year before, when Gretzky was getting NHL players' autographs for his kid brothers ...

One night when the New York Islanders were in town, goaltender Chico Resch asked Gretzky for his autograph.

"It's for my 15-year-old nephew," he told Gretzky. "He didn't want my autograph. He wanted yours."

The Leafs for Gretzky, and Moncton, too

In the first half of the season, there were those who were saying Gretzky wasn't having the year he had had in 1979-80 but, by the time the Boston Bruins and Toronto Maple Leafs had visited Edmonton in early January, the critics had been silenced — again.

Gretzky had been involved in 10 of the 11 goals the Oilers scored in the two-game series. In the previous year, after 40 games, Gretzky had 58 points. After the Boston and Toronto visits, the Oilers had played 37 games and Gretzky had 60 points.

Leafs' owner Harold Ballard made the trip to Edmonton to watch Gretzky do his usual number on the Leafs.

"I'd trade my whole team for Gretzky," said Ballard. "And I'd throw in Moncton, too.

"I might as well trade my whole team for him. If I got him, I'd have nobody to play with him anyhow."

Funny. That happened to be the Oilers' problem. They hadn't had anybody to play with Gretzky either. So far in the season Gretzky's wingers had been Dave Semenko, Don Murdoch, Brett Callighen, Jari Kurri, Blair MacDonald, Mark Messier, Glenn Anderson and Don Ashby.

"Gretzky has had a new winger just about every game," admitted coach Sather. "Every day, my number one priority as general manager is to find a goal scorer for Gretzky. We have to put somebody on that line who can score, and score every night. If I could find somebody, either in a trade or in the draft, who could score 50 or 60 goals, it would be heaven. The only thing I worry about in the meantime is that I'm going to burn him out.''

Was Gretzky struggling?

"Are you kidding?'' said Sather. "When you consider what he's had to put up with, he has been better this year. MUCH better.''

Callighen and Kurri would end up as Gretzky's regular line-mates the rest of the way. And as the season progressed, it would become a trifle obvious that he was having a much better season. Much better than anybody in hockey history.

Gretzky fit to be tied — with Marcel Dionne

The Oilers were in Quebec City when they completed the first half of their schedule. A five-point night from Gretzky had just propelled the Oilers to a 6-3 win over the Nordiques.

"Why do I think I've been down this road before?'' said Gretzky after the game.

The five points left Gretzky tied with Dionne at the half-season mark, each with 70 points. But Dionne had 10 more goals, so he won the half-season scoring race and the $500 prize money.

"After 120 games, I have the same number of points as Dionne, yet I've lost two scoring titles.''

A couple of weeks later, it was obvious that this would not be the case after 160 games.

First, the Oilers, led as always by Gretzky, scored what everybody was convinced would be the win of the year for the team. It was one of the most impressive "defeats" in the entire history of the greatest team in the history of hockey. The Oilers hammered the Montreal Canadiens 9-1.

"It was the thrill of a lifetime to beat Montreal 5-3 last year,'' said Gretzky, who led the way scoring five points.

"But this ...

"Well, I don't think they've ever been beaten like this in their entire history.''

To find a Montreal Canadiens' defeat such as the one the Edmonton Oilers administered, you had to go back to 1974 when the Canadiens lost 9-2 to the New York Rangers. That

Wayne is thwarted on a breakaway by Los Angeles Kings' netminder — but it's heads-up hockey all the way! (*BRIAN GAVRILOFF, EDMONTON JOURNAL*)

same year Montreal lost 8-0 to Boston. And there was a 10-2 loss to Chicago in 1970. But were 10-2, 9-2, and 8-0 defeats worse than a 9-1 loss to a team only a year and a half out of the World Hockey Association and the merger rape? No? Well then you had to go back to the 1943-44 season; Montreal lost 10-0 to Detroit that year.

"From a fan's point of view," said Gretzky in the post-game dressing room, "that has to be the biggest win we've ever had."

The Kid was rolling now. And exactly one month after the midway mark of the schedule, Gretzky finally passed Dionne.

Three goals and three assists against the Winnipeg Jets put Gretzky three points up on Dionne.

The gap would widen.

Making a move on the record book

Nobody had been mentioning it before, but now it was being noticed. The Kid had a shot at a couple of records that many people believed would never be broken.

In 1970-71, Bobby Orr recorded 102 assists. At his current pace Gretzky would end up with 104 assists.

And points? The record was Phil Esposito's 152 from the same season. Gretzky would end up with 151 if he kept scoring at his incredible rate.

Gretzky, who had been avoiding comment on the scoring race all season, was inspired to admit a few things after the Winnipeg game.

The Orr record, he said, fascinated him.

"If I'm ever going to break a record," he said, "that would be the one I'd want. I consider myself a playmaker more than a scorer. I don't consider myself a natural scorer."

And as for the scoring race?

"It will be different from here on in," predicted Gretzky. "Last year I played catch-up all the way in the scoring race. Now that I'm ahead, I think it will be easier on me."

But the scoring championship and records were not the only thing Gretzky had a shot at. He had a chance to win the Hart Trophy again. And by February 18th, when the St. Louis Blues came to Edmonton, it was more than obvious the battle for the Hart Trophy was down to two — Gretzky and St. Louis netminder Mike Liut.

Gretzky vs. Liut was obviously the way the game would be billed. And if one game can affect the voting for a season of play, this one did.

Gretzky played what many observers called his second or third greatest game in the NHL.

Five goals!

And two assists!

While setting Oiler NHL records for most goals in a game and fastest two, three, four and five goals in a game, Gretzky also tied a National Hockey League record for most goals in a single period — with Busher Jackson.

"Busher Jackson?" said the 20-year-old. "Who is that? He must have broken in before Gordie Howe, eh? I've never heard of 'The Busher'."

Gretzky was only one goal shy of equaling the NHL record of six goals in a game. If he had done it, he would have done it in front of the man who set the record, St. Louis coach Red Berenson.

"I remember Berenson getting that record," said The Kid. "I was eight that year. I was playing novice hockey then. But I remember it."

Watching that game was enough for one Hall of Famer to wave the white flag.

Goaltender Glenn Hall watched from the press box and when it was over he said he thought he'd faced the best, but now he knew one had come along who was better.

"Wayne Gretzky is the greatest hockey player I've ever seen," said Hall that night.

The Oilers won it 9-2 and Gretzky now led Dionne 112-105. And one couldn't help but think back to Walter Gretzky's prediction at the all-star game.

"He'll win by 22 points," said dad.

With 23 games to play, Gretzky needed 40 points to equal Esposito's record and 28 assists to equal Orr's.

"It's going to be close," said Gretzky after the game.

Gretzky chasing the records — that would obviously be the story-line for the rest of this season.

After the St. Louis game, Gretzky was averaging 1.96 points per game, barely behind Bill Cowley's record of 1.97 from 1943-44. He was now ahead of Esposito's pace.

In his past nine home games, Gretzky had 13 goals and 18 assists for 31 points. That was 3.4 points per game. In his past 17 games, home and away, he had 42 points. That was an average of 2.7 per game. Continue that pace and he'd break the records by a wide margin.

At this point you had to peek at his career totals. One more point and this lad who had just turned 20 would have NHL point number 250. He needed 11 goals for his 100th NHL goal. And 40 assists for his 200th NHL assist. And remember, Gretzky played a year in the WHA. His major league totals were 135 goals and 224 assists for 359 points. People were beginning to wonder if a player could come up with 500 major league points by his 21st birthday.

No crying in beer for Phil Esposito

The goals and assists kept coming. And now, around hockey, the controversy was raging. It was obvious that Gretzky would better Esposito's record. Would the accomplishment of Gretzky be as great as the decade-old record belonging to Esposito? Or would it be like inflation? A dollar isn't worth what a dollar was worth ten years ago and neither is a goal or an assist. That's the pro-Esposito argument. But Esposito, who generally doesn't walk away from controversy, wasn't arguing. Not even a little bit.

''He's one hell of a hockey player, that kid,'' said Espo. ''I can't think of anybody I'd rather have break the record than Wayne Gretzky.

''There's not going to be any controversial angle from Phil Esposito on this story. People are expecting me to be crying in my beer, or begrudge what Wayne has accomplished this year, but maybe they've forgotten a few things.

''Remember when I set the record? Everybody was saying I got all those goals and all those points because of expansion.

They didn't even name me the most valuable player. They didn't even give me the Hart Trophy. Now those same people are trying to put down· what Wayne has accomplished and all of a sudden my record is up on the pedestal. It's silliness.''

In 1970-71, when Esposito scored 76 goals and 76 assists, the Boston Bruins tallied an NHL record 399 goals. Esposito was involved in 38 percent of them. To this point, Gretzky had been involved in 50 percent of the Oiler scoring. Esposito had Bobby Orr and Wayne Cashman and Ken Hodge. Wayne Gretzky had nobody. Gretzky ended up exactly 89 points ahead of the second-most prolific Oiler, and that Oiler got a great many of his points as a result of Gretzky being on his line. The Oilers didn't win a single game in 1980-81 when Gretzky had been shut out. In two years of NHL play, Gretzky was shut out 30 times and the Oilers managed to win only one of those games.

''I'm not going to deny that stuff,'' said Espo. ''Wayne Gretzky means one heck of a lot more to the Edmonton Oilers than I meant to the Boston Bruins. For Wayne to do what he is doing with that team, you have to give him a lot of credit. It's not exactly the most well-kept secret in hockey that if you stop Gretzky, you stop the Oilers. I had Orr and Hodge and Cashman, and obviously Wayne doesn't have great players to play with.''

Pleau sparks new-line great debate
Unfortunately for a day or two, there would be controversy about the record.

In Hartford, on March 26, the Oilers scored three empty-net goals and won 7-2 as the Whalers tried in desperation to score with a sixth attacker and improve their dismal chances for a playoff spot. Gretzky, who earlier in the game was credited with an assist, scored one goal and added two more assists with the Whaler net empty. This sudden outburst gave him 151 points, now only one point behind Esposito's record.

In Boston, general manager Harry Sinden called it ''a farce.'' He said, ''I don't think it was proper,'' and added, ''I hope it doesn't detract from young Gretzky's accomplishment.''

Minnesota North Star coach Glen Sonmor said he had serious questions about the move by Pleau to leave the goaltender out with the score 5-2 and then 6-2. "Somebody should be asking Pleau about his reasoning."

Brian O'Neill, executive vice-president of the NHL, said it was "poor strategy" and a "foolish measure" and "not a very smart move," but the league planned no action against Pleau.

However, the man whose record stood to be broken said, "Big deal. He's going to get the record anyway. Over an entire season things even out and these sorts of things happen a lot."

Gretzky? He was avoiding all controversy.

"Anytime you come close to any records of any sort," said Gretzky, "it's on your mind. Considering it's Esposito's, I'm honored to be coming close to him. I was only eight or nine years old when he was going good."

The Oiler center was scoring at an unprecedented 2.01 points-per-game clip. And everybody was converging on Detroit to watch him break it the next time out. "I've got three tickets for my mom, dad, and little brother," said Gretzky, "and there are four or five hundred other people that I know who are driving down to see the game."

Wayne Gretzky: King of the NHL
Gretzky tied Esposito's record in Detroit with a pass to Risto Siltanen in a 4-2 win over the Red Wings. The following evening in Pittsburgh he assisted on goals by Mark Messier, Brent Callighen, and Jari Kurri in a game that the Oilers won 5-2. The three assists not only helped Gretzky clear the Esposito record with a whopping 155 points, but gave him 102 assists which tied him with Bobby Orr for the most assists in a season.

"I'm happy and relieved to get it over with," said Gretzky, who had surpassed Esposito with a 24-point spree in his past ten games (20 assists, 4 goals).

Gretzky had said before the season that all he wanted to do was improve on his 137 points of the previous year, but he did have a distant goal in mind: "I wanted two points per game if I could get it because no one has ever done that before."

Well, one guy had come close.

Bill Cowley, a 69-year-old Hall of Famer, owned the only record left for Gretzky to shoot for now. Cowley had the

(BRIAN GAVRILOFF, EDMONTON JOURNAL)

"Highest Points Per Game Average One Season (among players with 50 points or more in one season) Record." He scored 71 points in 36 games with the Boston Bruins in 1943-44 for a 1.97 average. If Gretzky could come up with 5 points in his last three games, he'd become the first NHL player to average two points per game.

"Two points a game over an 80-game schedule," said Cowley, "that would be amazing. I never thought I'd see the day when a player would do that. I always thought that would be impossible.

"They forgot old Bill Cowley a long time ago. But they'll never forget Wayne Gretzky."

Cowley said, to be quite honest about it, that he didn't think much of his own record.

"I didn't even know I had the record until ten years after I finished my career and even then it was my son who found it in some program at some game he was at in some other town."

Cowley didn't figure the writers would stumble on it as they searched the record book for the damage Gretzky had done this year.

"A week or so before he broke Esposito's record my wife said the phone would start ringing from reporters, but I said nobody would notice and if they did they wouldn't make much of it."

Cowley wasn't putting down Gretzky's accomplishments or the record category. "For someone to average two points a game over an 80-game schedule, well, that's about as impressive a mark as you can make in hockey as far as I'm concerned. It's just that I never felt MY name should have been in the book. I only played 36 games that year. I don't think 36 games should have rated that record. I've been waiting for the day when the NHL would whitewash my record out of the book. I've been waiting for the day when the NHL would say, 'Let's get rid of that Cowley record because he didn't play enough games.' "

In the Oilers' 78th game, a 4-4 tie with Colorado, Gretzky got the one point he really wanted, the one that broke the supposedly impossible-to-break assist record of Bobby Orr. Gretzky set up Jari Kurri twice in the game to do it.

Orr played 78 games with Boston in the 1970-71 season to establish his assists record. Gretzky surpassed Orr in the same number of games and had picked up 22 assists in the past nine games to do it. Wayne said, ''I really wanted to do it tonight so that nobody could complain I had done it in more games.''

The Oilers finished the season off by hammering the Winnipeg Jets 7-2 to end up in 14th place and Gretzky wound up with the best individual season of all time with a goal (number 55) and four more assists for an incredible 164 points. That's 12 more points than Esposito, 7 more assists than Orr, and his average points per game worked out to 2.05, .08 better than Cowley. And Dionne was 29 points back.

Gretzky actually bettered his father's prediction at the all-star break when he led Dionne by only four points.

''I would never have bet on me getting that many points,'' admitted Wayne. ''I really thought the team could finish where we did. You have to improve a little bit each year . . . next year it will be tenth place.''

The youngest player before Gretzky to win the NHL scoring title was Busher Jackson who won it at the age of 21 in 1931-32. Busher had 28 goals and 25 assists for 53 points in 48 games.

Gretzky earned 94 points in the second half of the season surpassing the record of 87 set by center Stan Mikita of the Chicago Black Hawks in 1967-68, the season the NHL went from six to twelve teams.

''If Wayne Gretzky is not the league's most valuable player again, the guys picking them are retards,'' said Oiler coach Glen Sather. ''Wayne Gretzky is the best thing hockey has seen in the last decade.''

''They play with no nerves.''

The voting for the NHL awards wouldn't be announced until June and it was now on to the playoffs for Gretzky and the Oilers. If there were any doubters left after the regular season, Gretzky took care of them in the first game of the Stanley Cup playoffs.

It was in the Montreal Forum. And against the Montreal

Canadiens in what some people believed might have been Gretzky's greatest game. There had already been so many it was tough to say. Five assists to tie a Stanley Cup record. Three assists in the first period to tie another one.

To everyone Gretzky was the story. But The Kid pointed to the corner of the dressing room and correctly labelled Andy Moog as *the story*.

Coach Glen Sather had taken a gamble and started a kid named Andy Moog in goal, and The Kid at center was marvelling at his overnight co-star.

"Honestly," said Gretzky, "Andy Moog is the most confident twenty-year-old I've ever met."

Moog, who broke into the NHL by allowing a goal on the first shot he faced fourteen weeks earlier in Los Angeles, flipped and flopped and stopped twenty-eight of thirty-one shots as the Oilers won 6-3 and took game one of the best-of-five preliminary series.

Moog wanted to get through with his post-game interviews as quickly as possible so he could get to a telephone. "I can't wait to phone home to Penticton," he said.

And what would his first words be? "Hey, look what I did."

"What an honor!" raved Paul Coffey, another member of the Kiddie Corps, who was starring at the end of the season. "To beat the Montreal Canadiens in the Forum, in the Stanley Cup playoffs. I can't think of a better word. What an honor!"

"What an unbelievable thrill," said Kevin Lowe. "I'm a hero. A Stanley Cup hero."

When the Oilers won the NEXT game 3-1, there was shock in the face of every fan who was there. Those faces were different from the year before when the Minnesota North Stars won three games in the Forum and knocked the Canadiens out of the playoffs in the second round. It was disbelief when Minnesota did it: shock and horror was more the way to describe them this year.

The Oilers were still children. Didn't they realize who they were playing? Didn't they understand?

This series was supposed to be experience vs. inexperience. For the Oiler kids, the youngest team in the NHL in 1980-81, this was to be kind of a field trip to play the Canadiens in the Forum in the Stanley Cup playoffs ... Maybe something would rub off for the future. What it really was, was young legs vs. old legs. The Oilers outskated the Canadiens, they worked harder, and they showed more desire. Experience hadn't meant a thing unless you were talking about the Oilers' experience against Philadelphia in the playoffs a year earlier.

The Oilers had not been intimidated by the rink, by the uniform, by the history, or by anything.

"They play with no nerves," said Canadiens' coach Claude Ruel.

"Maybe we're so young that we're naive," said Oiler captain Lee Fogolin.

After game one the Oilers were saying what an honor it had been to win a playoff game in the Forum, but they went out in game two and played the Canadiens as if they were the next team in the regular season schedule.

"The thing we did was remind ourselves that we'd seen teams win the first playoff game against Montreal and then lose all the rest," said Wayne Gretzky. "We just went out there and tried to do the same things we did the night before. We reminded ourselves that they have all the pressure. We don't have any pressure at all unless we put it on ourselves, so why get uptight? We made up our minds to come here and give it everything we could give."

The Oilers did exactly that and Andy Moog, who in 27 hours went from a nobody to a household name, did the rest.

"Do you think anybody in the NHL believes us?" bubbled Gretzky on the flight home. "Do you, huh? Do you?"

He had company.

"This is Fantasy Island," crowed defenceman Paul Coffey.

What had happened to Montreal? Why were they in this unbelievable jam?

"In a word," said Yvon Lambert, "Gretzky."

"All we've been doing is panicking whenever Gretzky is on the ice," said Keith Acton. "We have guys on this team who are superstars too. We've got to get Edmonton worrying about them instead of us just worrying about Gretzky."

The Gretzky and Moog Show

The scene that greeted the Oilers when they arrived home for game three at the Northlands Coliseum was one they would not soon forget.

On one side of the Coliseum hung a sign that read: "We believe in miracles." On the other side sat a fan in a Montreal Canadiens' jacket with a bag over his head. Between the two it said it all, if you *could* say it all about what had happened to the Oilers and to Edmonton in a span of four days.

And when the Oilers won game three 6-2 to sweep the series that night, you could have called it one of the greatest upsets in Stanley Cup history — maybe The Greatest Upset when you consider it was a 14th place club, a team of mere children, a club only two years out of the World Hockey Association ... The team they beat was more than a third-place club; it was the legendary Montreal Canadiens.

One. Two. Three. In total goals it was fifteen to six.

It was intoxicating, perhaps the greatest single sporting thrill in Edmonton history. Wayne Gretzky and Andy Moog were the stars of it all. Gretzky figured in eleven of the Oilers' goals. And Moog, a kid with only six games of NHL experience, and the 132nd pick in the NHL draft, was equally outstanding.

But what of the rest of the kids? The Oilers went into the series as underdogs. To get into the playoffs, it was mostly Gretzky. Nobody else rated more than a "half share." But in the series, every regular played up to his ability. And the key to it all, as much as it was Gretzky, and as much as it was Moog, was probably the third line. Going into the playoffs, the Oilers were at best a two-line hockey club. Their third line was so bad the Oilers were the hockey equivalent of Spahn and Sain and Pray For Rain. But they did it, and the whole club rated a full share for the playoff story of the season.

Hard knocks by the Stanley Cup champs

When the Oilers arrived in Uniondale, New York, the first thing they noticed was that only one Stanley Cup pennant hung from the ceiling, not twenty-two.

But it was the most recent pennant, and the Islanders,

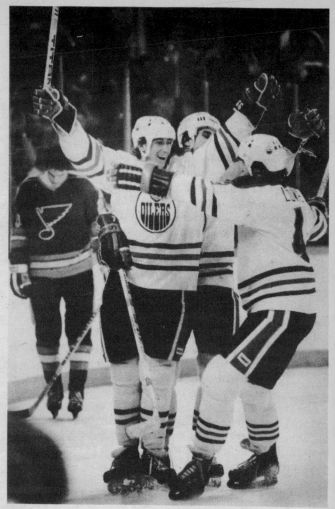

Another goal *(BRIAN GAVRILOFF, EDMONTON JOURNAL)*

according to a headline in the *New York Post*, did not like Wayne Gretzky's attitude coming off the Montreal series.

ISLES HOPE TO MAKE GRETZKY EAT HIS WORDS

screamed the largest sports headline in the edition. The article underneath it quoted Gretzky as having said, "We had to beat the best team in hockey to get here."

"That ticks me off," Bob Nystrom was quoted in the *Post*. "If he considers Montreal the best team in hockey, we'll just have to go out there and show him he's wrong."

"It's always good to hear somebody say that," Stefan Persson was quoted as saying. "The Canadiens were the greatest team in hockey but not now. I think Gretzky's got it backwards."

You didn't have to paint a picture for the Oilers to know how the Islanders felt. But when the series opened, somebody *was* painting a picture. Wayne Gretzky by this point had been viewed in just about every way possible, but now he was being viewed as an art form.

LeRoy Neiman, the internationally famous artist who stands among contemporary artists in capturing the color, spectacle, and excitement of sport, sat beside the Oiler players bench in the Nassau County Coliseum sketching Gretzky prior to attempting to capture his artistry on canvas.

"He's hard to draw," was Neiman's first reaction.

"He's always someplace else."

Someplace else. That's as close to a perfect description as you are going to find of the way Wayne Gretzky plays the game.

Neiman's painting was a commissioned work. It was a business deal which, perhaps better than any of the long list of endorsements the Edmonton superstar has been offered, illustrates the current marketability of The Kid.

The Michael Barnett Agency of Vancouver put up $400,000 for one original painting which would go to the agency; three copies, one each for Gretzky, his dad, his agent; and 300 serigraphs which would be sold for $4,000 each.

"We got the number one sports artist in the world and Canada's number one athlete," said Barnett.

Gretzky made $50,000 for autographing the 300 serigraphs.

Gretzky as an art form?

"I'd never seen him play before," said Neiman, the official artist of the last two Olympic games.

"One of the most important things was to see how he skated. The thing I noticed right off was the comparison to Gordie Howe. Gordie was so erect. This guy is erect most of the time as well.

"Like I said, he's really difficult to draw. Most hockey players you can capture right in front of the net. But this guy is all over the place. Another thing is that he's not filled out yet and when he puts his helmet on he loses a lot of his identity. I remember sketching Ted Lindsay once. He was a delight to draw. He was all banged up. Wayne does not have any teeth knocked out and he is not all banged up."

Was Neiman staring at a blank canvas? "No," said Neiman. "What you really work on is the cleanness. That's the thing that struck me most. He's really got something, the way he plays, that I have never seen before. And it's the cleanness of his style. As I sat beside him on the bench, I also noticed another thing about him. I have never seen a player as locked into the game as he is, even when he's sitting on the bench.

"But the other thing I really have to capture is the 'How-can-anybody-that-young-be-that-good?'."

While Neiman was sketching, the Oilers returned to their paint-by-numbers regular season style of hockey and lost 6-3 and 8-2 to the Islanders for openers.

But back home on Easter Sunday, it was the Oilers' official day of confirmation. The Oilers won 5-2 and for the moment were back in the series.

And once again, this was a study. For the Edmonton Oilers this was the most memorable moment in their history.

"With the Montreal series, and so far in this series, I'd say we have matured at least a full year as a hockey team in a span of less than three weeks," said Gretzky, who scored his second hat trick in the playoffs to inspire the victory.

"It must be nice for the fans to come out to the rink and see twenty guys working every night," Gretzky continued. "I think they can expect that in the regular seasons from now on."

Gretzky had been twenty going on thirty-five for some time

now. And Andy Moog had been something of a Gretzky in goal pads since all of this started. The game's story as the Oilers came back to win game three was the same as it had been in each Oiler playoff victory so far: Gretzky. And goaltending. But once again it was not by any means the whole story.

"The thing I can't believe," said captain Lee Fogolin, "is the young guys. It's hard to explain. They're so young. Too young to feel pressure. They are getting so good together. All at once. Every day. From one game to the next game. From one day to the next day. It's just fantastic. At the start of all of this, we were a second-year NHL team. But we're not anymore because of everything that's happened. It's like we've been around much longer than that now."

The Oilers were outstanding at home in game four, taking the Islanders into overtime. The defending Stanley Cup champions avoided going home tied at two games with a sudden-death goal by Ken Morrow.

When the fans left the Coliseum after game four, they felt it finally had to be over for those Cardiac Kids. Surely they had run out of miracles.

The Edmonton Boys Choir

When the series returned to Uniondale for game five, it was abundantly clear that there had never been a team in the Stanley Cup playoffs quite like *this* one.

Gretzky and goaltending. That was the story-line. But you couldn't ignore the rest of the kids on the Oilers, either. They'd come a long way this season. And the scene was every bit as much theirs as it was Gretzky's or Moog's.

Four minutes remained in game five and the Edmonton Oilers sitting on the bench were singing. *Singing!*

"Here we go Oilers, Here we go ... Here we go ... Here we go Oilers, Here we go."

In Montreal, Canadiens' coach Claude Ruel had said, "They have no nerves." But singing on the bench in Long Island?

"This is getting to be fun," said defenceman Kevin Lowe.

"Every time we got in trouble, we started singing," said coach Glen Sather, shaking his head.

"Teenagers," marvelled assistant coach Billy Harris.

If singing on the bench wasn't enough, they were also singing in their dressing room between the second and third periods.

"I think it was Mark Messier who started it," said Paul Coffey. "It just felt right to start singing. We don't know how to be goodie-goodies yet. We're a young team. We don't know how to sit there and take it all in stride."

What had happened was indeed unbelievable. A second-year NHL team. Seven players young enough to be playing in the junior Memorial Cup. Upsetting the Montreal Canadiens in three straight! Two wins in the Montreal Forum! And now a win on The Island! And taking the Stanley Cup champions to a sixth game . . .

The Oilers were outshot 23-12 in the last two periods, but Moog was spectacular and the Oilers won it 4-3.

"What it comes down to," said Gretzky, who set up two more goals for his 19th and 20th points in eight playoff games, "is that we're just going out there and trying to work as hard as they do. We're trying to be just as physical as they are. I know I've never been hit this much in my life. It's just amazing how loose we are, considering we're down 3-2. It's proof of what everybody is saying. We're too young to know what pressure is. We're the youngest team in the NHL. Just a bunch of kids. And what we're doing is saying to ourselves: 'Let's just give it our best shot.' It's wrong to say we're going to beat them. And we're not going to say that. All we're saying is that we've got nothing to lose. We're going to go back out and give it our best shot again."

As Gretzky spoke, from out of the showers came the song again.

"Here we go, Oilers, here we go . . ."

Midnight finally comes for Cinderella Oilers

Back in Edmonton for game six, the Islanders prevailed and won what would prove to be their only tough series on the way to a second straight Stanley Cup.

The Oilers were out of the Stanley Cup playoffs. But for most Canadian hockey fans this year, Gretzky, Moog, and the Oilers MADE the Stanley Cup playoffs.

And unlikely as it may sound, the Islanders, too, had been

captivated with the Oilers. It was a mutual admiration society in the dressing rooms when it was over.

While the mob of reporters interviewed coach Al Arbour in the hall outside the visitors dressing room, the Islanders, with big grins on their faces inside the room, began to sing a revised edition of the Oilers' hit song from the game before.

"Here we go Islanders, here we go ..."

"I've never been in a series like this one," said Islander captain Denis Potvin. "It was more than a classic Stanley Cup playoff series. It was a series based almost entirely on emotion. It wasn't like playing Philadelphia or Montreal. It wasn't normal like that. It was all based on emotion and desire. It was tough to play them. They were all over the ice. They made it so frustrating. And now that it's over, we're more relieved than anything."

"They were like a snowball," said Bryan Trottier. "They were rolling and they just kept getting bigger and bigger. They were doing things you don't see young teams do. They certainly didn't lack enthusiasm. It was weird playing them. It was like we were playing ourselves of five years ago."

Bob Nystrom said that of all the Islanders, he believed he'd be the last guy to praise another team.

"I'm not one to dole out compliments," he said, "but they were tremendous."

Wayne Gretzky, who ended with seven goals and 14 assists for 21 points in nine playoff games — the highest total of any player who didn't make it to the Stanley Cup final, and the only player who played less than ten games to score more than 12 playoff points — was left to put it in perspective.

"The most important thing we did was to create a winning attitude here," he said. "The Edmonton Eskimos don't know how to lose. We lost the series, but hopefully we also lost, forever, the droopy kind of attitude we had. Hopefully we'll start to show a lot more in the regular season from now on. We didn't play intense hockey during the season. Now, when a player comes to this team, he'll have to adopt the attitude that is here."

Midnight finally came for Gretzky, Moog, and the Miracle Oilers of the 1981 Stanley Cup playoffs. But the sun would shine on them all summer.

Soon to be hockey's highest paid?

It was during the Stanley Cup final series, in Bloomington, Minnesota, when Gretzky broke the news — the Oilers had agreed to renegotiate his contract.

"They came to me," said Gretzky, who was at the final to receive the award as NHL Player of the Year. "They've opened the door and here we go."

Gretzky was not offering any false modesty at this point.

"I'd like to be the highest-paid player in the National Hockey League," he said.

But he also made it clear that he had no desire to get out of the clause in the original contract which would keep him an Oiler until 1999.

"I don't want to leave Edmonton. I'm happy the Oilers have come to me and suggested renegotiation. I wasn't in a position, really, to go to them. The next renegotiation clause in my contract isn't for five or six years. But I would have been a little disappointed if they hadn't come to me.

"I think the timing is just about right. I've played three years for the Oilers now. I think I've proved myself. Anybody can have a great three weeks or great three months, but three years is pretty good proof.

"They've treated me well and I've treated them well. They know my value and I know my value."

What was Gretzky making?

Only $150,000 a season.

"I make twice as much money in the off-season as I do in the hockey season. That one 7-Up commercial is worth $100,000. That's two-thirds of my salary."

The Kid's all Hart again — MVP 099

About the time it was being announced that Gretzky had been named Hart Trophy winner as the NHL's Most Valuable Player for the second year in a row, a set of licence plates were being placed on a 1961 Cadillac convertible.

The licence number: MVP 099.

Jeff Landry of Morinville, Alberta, had spent three years reconditioning the car, the exact length of time Gretzky had been in Edmonton. Only a couple of weeks earlier, Landry registered the Caddy. And finally, he was putting the plates on it — the very day when Gretzky was named MVP — when somebody noticed.

"Somebody in my shop brought it to my attention," he said of the plates which were regular issue. "I didn't even know what I had. I think it looks pretty good on the car. After all, 1961 was the year Wayne was born. And he most certainly is a Cadillac."

At 42 Varadi Avenue in Brantford, Walter Gretzky laughed.

"I know you are going to think I'm crazy, but I'm convinced Wayne's life was planned a long time ago. The things that have happened . . .

"A guy in Edmonton draws an MVP 099 licence plate number and puts it on his car, a Cadillac from the same year Wayne was born, the same day Wayne wins the MVP . . .

"It's like when Wayne tied Phil Esposito's record at 1:52 of the period and it was exactly 1:52 P.M. in Edmonton when he did it.

"I'm not even surprised at any of that stuff anymore. I really am convinced his life was planned a long time ago."

One thing that was planned a long time ago was that Wayne was going to let his dad keep all his awards.

"Even when I'm 40, they'll still go to my father," said Wayne. "I think he's more proud of them than I am."

The Kid, The Flower, and the Canada Cup

While all of this was going on, there was planning for the Canada Cup. And early in summer, people were beginning to speculate, as one headline put it, that there might be "Flower Power for The Kid?".

Gretzky was trying to be non-committal when people asked him who he wanted to play with in the Canada Cup.

"Um, oh . . . it doesn't really matter," he said.

But in the next breath somebody would mention the name Guy Lafleur and Gretzky would have a direct question to deal with.

"Well, I'd be honored if I got the chance to play alongside The Flower," Gretzky would say. "I guess I'd love to play with Guy Lafleur for sentimental reasons. It's just like when I got to

(BRIAN GAVRILOFF, EDMONTON JOURNAL)

play with Gordie Howe against the Soviets a few years ago.''

Gretzky knew the lay of the land going into the Cup.

''This is the first time I've gone into a season without people saying I wouldn't and I couldn't,'' he said. ''But if I bomb out in this series, people are going to say I was lucky the last two seasons.''

On August 10th, for openers at least, Gretzky and The Flower were on the same line

Team Canada coach Scotty Bowman made the announcement as training camp opened.

''Gretzky will play with Lafleur and Steve Shutt,'' he said.

Lafleur reacted with a smile.

''It will be a lot easier to play with him than against him. I've watched him play and I think he's a great hockey player. It will be great to have a chance to play with him.''

When Team Canada arrived in Edmonton to play the Soviets in their final exhibition game, after much line juggling along the way, it was Gretzky, Lafleur, and Gil Perreault.

And the scene was magic in the Northlands Coliseum.

Gretzky's new line-mate was welcomed like he never expected.

All night the fans — who had occasionally booed Lafleur in the past, as fans will do to great hockey players who play for the visiting teams — chanted ''Guy, Guy, Guy.''

''I didn't expect that,'' said Lafleur. ''Maybe it's the Edmonton fans' way of saying thank you for what happened last spring.''

Gretzky with Lafleur was a dream.

''Wayne is doing everything,'' said Lafleur after Team Canada won the game. ''Gilbert and I are still rushing things. We don't have good timing yet. Tonight, with the right timing, I could have had three of four goals set up by Wayne. I've never played with anybody who can do what he can do. When he's behind the net, it has to be tough on the Russians. They've never played against anybody who plays the game he does from behind the net.''

The Soviets? They claimed not to be so impressed.

Goaltender Vladislav Tretiak called Gretzky a typical European player. ''He doesn't like to go in the corners and he doesn't like to play rough.''

''For us,'' said team spokesman Vladimir Yurzinov, ''it is easy to play against Wayne Gretzky. He plays the Soviet style. He's very close to our style of play so it is easy to play against him.''

Yurzinov said he was familiar with The Kid, though, and that he was good.

''We saw Gretzky when he was in the WHA. He is an unusual player. He's dangerous to any kind of team. Behind the net, he's dangerous twice.''

Gretzky admitted he couldn't believe his eyes with what he saw in the exhibition game with the Soviets.

''I noticed I had a lot of freedom behind the net. I expect them to play me a little different the next time. But I don't know ... All I know right now is what a joy it is to play with everybody here.''

After one look at Gretzky with his Team Canada team-mates, his regular season coach, Glen Sather, was prepared to make a prediction about how it was going to be.

''I think I wondered if he'd find his level in the Canada Cup,'' said Sather. ''Everybody saw it tonight. He was head and shoulders above anybody else on the ice. After watching him tonight, I don't have any doubt about him finding a level now. I think it's going to be his show.''

It was already his show. Wayne Gretzky was everybody's cover boy for the Canada Cup. It was his Canada Cup and whatever happened, yea or nay, it was going to be that way.

The first major setback of a career

For the most part, it was yea.

Gretzky was the top point-getter in the entire tournament. Twice, in the game against Sweden and in the game against Russia, he won Labatt's soapstone carvings as Team Canada's Most Valuable Player.

For the most part it was magic.

But in the end ...

In the end, the Soviets won the final 8-1.

Wayne Gretzky, like almost all of his team-mates, did not

play well. He was, in the end, a Canada Cup goat. He wasn't there when it counted. And who would ever forget the fifth Soviet goal? Gretzky gave the puck away at the Soviet blue line. Guy Lafleur shied away from a fake shot and could only watch as the Soviet swept around him for a clear path to the net. And it was as though goaltender Mike Liut wasn't even there for the shot. That one goal summarized the entire evening.

"It was a strange feeling," said Gretzky. "You wanted to look at it as just another hockey game. But there was no way to rationalize the feeling that you let the whole country down. I just went and hid for five days. My parents didn't even know where I went."

Gretzky said the experience was probably good for him.

"It was the first real setback of my career," he said. "Everything in my lifetime has gone my way. Everything has gone well.

"It proved I have a lot to learn. But I'm only 20 and I'm sure I'll have another Canada Cup.

"I don't believe I'll have to spend 80 games trying to live down the one game in the Canada Cup. I think people finally believe I can play in the NHL."

That they do. By his 32nd game of the 1981-82 season, Gretzky had scored 33 goals and has 46 assists for a total of 79 points. He leads the NHL scoring race by 25 points and is scoring at a clip that would give him 197 points on the season if he maintains his current pace.

Wayne Gretzky — who would turn 21 in January of 1982 — would now head into the "adult" stage of his career.

The question no longer was: "Is Gretzky Great?"

The only question that remains is: "Can The Great Gretzky survive the test of time . . .

"And become The Greatest?"

THE STATISTICAL RECORD

GRETZKY, WAYNE (GRETZ-kee)

Born, Brantford, Ont., January 26, 1961.
Center. Shoots left. 5' 11", 165 lbs.
Last amateur club: Sault St. Marie Greyhounds (Jrs.)

Season	Club	Lea	Regular Schedule					Playoffs				
			GP	G	A	TP	PIM	GP	G	A	TP	PIM
1978-79	Indianapolis	WHA	8	3	3	6	0	....	....	....	....	....
1978-79	Edmonton	WHA	72	43	61	104	19	13	*10	10	*20	2
1979-80 abc	Edmonton	NHL	79	51	*86	*137	21	3	2	1	3	0
1980-81 ade fg	Edmonton	NHL	80	55	*109	*164	28	9	7	14	21	4
	NHL Totals		159	106	195	301	49	12	9	15	24	4
	WHA Totals		80	46	64	110	19	13	10	10	20	2

*Establishes new record

A. Won Hart Trophy.
B. Won Lady Byng Trophy.
C. Second All-Star Team (center).
D. First All-Star Team (center).
E. Won Art Ross Trophy.
F. NHL record for assists in regular season.
G. NHL record for points in regular season.
Reclaimed by Edmonton as an under-age junior prior to Expansion Draft, June 9, 1979.
Claimed as priority selection by Edmonton, June 9, 1979.